Christian Wenz
Tobias Hauser

IN NO TIME

HTML

Prentice
Hall

An imprint of Pearson Education

PEARSON EDUCATION LIMITED

Head Office:
Edinburgh Gate
Harlow CM20 2JE
Tel: +44 (0)1279 623623
Fax: +44 (0)1279 431059

London Office:
128 Long Acre
London WC2E 9AN
Tel: +44 (0)20 7447 2000
Fax: +44 (0)20 7240 5771

First published in Germany in 2001
© Pearson Education Limited 2002

First published in 2001 as *Easy HTML*
by Markt & Technik Buch-und Software-Verlag GmbH
Martin-Kollar-Straße 10-12
D-81829 Munich
Germany

This edition published 2002 by Pearson Education

British Library Cataloguing in Publication Data
A CIP catalogue record for this book can be obtained from the British Library.

ISBN 0-130-94938-8

10   9   8   7   6   5   4   3   2   1

Translated and typeset by Cybertechnics, Sheffield.
Printed and bound in Great Britian by Ashford Colour Press, Gosport, Hampshire.

The Publishers' policy is to use paper manufactured from sustainable forests.

Contents

Preface

Laudant illa, sed ista legunt.
People praise one thing, but choose to read another.

It is not clear whether Martial's accusation (Epigram 4,49,10) refers to hypocritical readers or authors with a bad reputation. However, we want to avoid both situations in this book. You should read this book and be able to admit it, because after reading it you will be able to create terrific HTML pages. We want you to have fun and learn as much as possible during the course of the book, so that you enjoy reading it and recommend it to other people.

To achieve this, the book is compiled in the following way: We begin with a chapter which introduces the topic of HTML – what HTML is and what you can do with it. This is followed by eleven chapters dealing extensively with HTML.

Throughout the text, we use boxes to give you notes and advice or point out problem areas.

Note

This box gives you additional information and important notes.

Tip

This box indicates shortcuts, and also gives tips and tricks for working with HTML.

> **Caution**
>
> *This box warns you about potential problems or things which you must be careful about.*

With most programming code in this book, lines are too long for the page and thus sentences have to be broken down. This will be shown using a special symbol.

```
Even if this sentence is broken down you should
Λ ignore the line break.
```

Thanks

We now want to thank two people: our lecturer Marcus Beck for his support, and our subject lecturer Ingo Dellwig for all the good work.

Starnberg, February 2001

Chapter 1

Brief Introduction

This chapter is not called "Brief Introduction" for nothing. First of all, you find out what HTML actually is. After this, we show you which software products you need in order to be able to understand the examples in this book. There will be no programming in this chapter; we will simply lay the foundation for the following eleven exercise units.

What is HTML?

The title and topic of this book is HTML. As you probably already know, Web sites are created in HTML. HTML is the abbreviation for *Hypertext Mark-up Language*. Contrary to popular opinion, it is not a programming language, but a page description language. HTML only describes how a Web site has to look; the Web browser takes control of the exact layout.

Imagine the following order of events: a browser requests an HTML page from a Web server. The server sends this page to the browser and the browser then contains an HTML file. This file must *interpret* this. This means that it analyses the content of the file and tries to display it the way the author of the page would like it to be displayed.

As we have already said, HTML is a page description language. An HTML file contains text as well as instructions on how to format this text (we discuss graphics later in the book). There are, for example, headings, unordered lists, and tables, all of which are itemised in the next chapter.

If you look at an HTML file, you will see elements which are written in pointed brackets, for example `<HTML>`. The following code:

```
<HTML>
<HEAD>
<TITLE>HTML</TITLE>
</HEAD>
<BODY BGCOLOR="WHITE">
<H1>Welcome to HTML!</H1>
</BODY>
</HTML>
```

is shown in Microsoft Internet Explorer as seen in Figure 1.1.

Figure 1.1: The file in Microsoft Internet Explorer

In the main competitor browser, Netscape Navigator, the page looks slightly different, as shown in Figure 1.2.

Figure 1.2: The file in Netscape Navigator

So you see that the same code is displayed differently in different browsers, which is why you must make sure of two things. You should:

- Install as many different browsers as possible on to your test system.
- Test your pages in as many possible browsers as possible.

On the Web some pages are 'optimised' for a specific type of browser. However, what may be acceptable for private use is a catastrophe for professional use. A third of all visitors view Web sites that are not displayed correctly because they use the 'incorrect' browser. The companies running such Web sites want to sell something but will not allow themselves to be arrogant in only developing for one browser; they test their sites using all browsers.

One would hope that the attitude "I only develop for my favourite browser" was no longer widespread; from several recent conferences we must conclude that there are more and more (alleged) professional Web developers who test their pages in only one browser. This is not professional and is a painful process.

A second problem with doing this is that one takes one's system as a measure of everything. A development computer is normally well-equipped with a large monitor, and good screen resolution. All files are on the hard disk, and are thus loaded quickly. However, this will not please a Web surfer who tries to look at the same pages on his laptop computer which has a low resolution and slow modem connection.

Our conclusion: test! Test Web sites with different browsers along the way, with different computers, ask friends and acquaintances to examine and criticise your site. In this volume we can only lay the foundations and give a couple of important tips and tricks, but the real design of the page lies in your hands.

Browsers

The first commercially successful Web browser was Netscape Navigator. It was also, for a long time, the only browser to be taken seriously until Microsoft jumped on to the Internet band wagon. Together with the operating system Windows 95, Internet Explorer 3.0 appeared in 1996 (the first viable version), and yet the dominance of Netscape was still unbroken.

The downfall of Netscape was slow. The company was bought out by AOL (America OnLine) and internal quarrelling prevented the rapid development of browsers. Only updates and bug fixes were produced. Internet Explorer, in comparison, produced several new versions, and the connection of the browser with the Microsoft operating system led to a rapid distribution. Because a large proportion of browsers are loaded in the memory during the booting of Windows, the program starts more quickly than its Netscape counterpart. In the meantime, Internet Explorer is clearly the leader according to the browser statistics.

The new Netscape version carries the number 6 (version 5 was skipped), and uses Open Source. This means that the source code can be seen freely, and any user can make a contribution to this browser. This will probably only last for a while, until the dominance in this area is able to be seriously threatened by Microsoft again.

Number 3 on the browser market, Opera, also deserves a mention. This browser only requires a fraction of the memory space that the other browsers require, is relatively fast, and for some time (like its competitors) was available free of charge. It can, however, be slow, and in the medium or even long term will not endanger the market share of the two browser giants.

> **Tip**
>
> *Before we turn to the installation and features of the individual browsers, here is another tip: most computer magazines pack current browser versions on to the CD-ROMs on their front covers. Before you download the whole package from the Internet, find out whether you already have this or another browser.*

Microsoft Internet Explorer

Microsoft Internet Explorer is delivered as standard, with the operating systems of the same manufacturer. However, versions also exist for the Apple Macintosh and (in a beta version) for Unix/Linux. The current printing version is 5.5sp1; there is already a beta from version 6.0 which will be delivered with the new operating system Windows XP.

The current version of the browser can also be downloaded from `http://www.microsoft.com/windows/IE`. The installation is run by the menu; it is best to use the standard installation (see Figure 1.3). The installation program itself is very small (about 500 KB), and the remaining software components are transferred to the Internet during the installation. After a reboot, the browser is available for use.

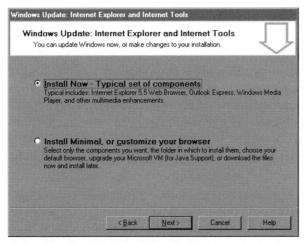

Figure 1.3: The types of installation: typical or customized

The automatic product updates are a special feature. They are combined with the update pages of Microsoft under the menu item TOOLS/WINDOWS UPDATE. Click on PRODUCT UPDATES and you can obtain convenient product updates. Not only updates of the browsers themselves are available here, but often updates of the operating systems as well. Click on the individual check boxes next to the desired product and then on DOWNLOAD. The only small disadvantage of this technology is that updates must be fully downloaded when using new browser versions.

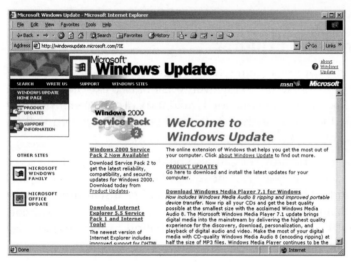

Figure 1.4: Microsoft Windows Update

Netscape Navigator

Netscape Navigator exists in two versions. The most up-to-date (and of course most stable) Windows version is Netscape 6. You can obtain this version from `http://home.netscape.com/download/0402101/10004-uk-win32-6.01-base-128_qual.html`. Here, you can also find versions for other operating systems. Netscape Navigator is available for most of the operating systems, including Apple Macintosh, Linux and diverse Unix versions.

During installation (here again, it is best to choose the default installation), there is a small peculiarity: at some point, the installation program asks you whether Netscape should be the default program for some applications (see Figure 1.5).

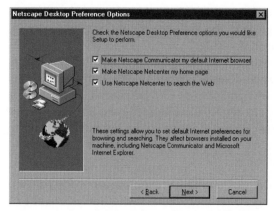

Figure 1.5: Netscape wants to be the default program

When you tick the check boxes here, it could cause conflicts between Netscape Navigator and Internet Explorer which can lead to problems. You should therefore deactivate these check boxes.

Following a successful installation, you can also load this browser over a Web interface. To do so, call up the menu item GO/NETSCAPE 6. Here you can download browser updates as well as additional software. The advantage of this is that with new versions of browser servers you don't have to transfer the whole of the software, but keep only the components. The disadvantage is that you have to register with Netscape (free of charge) in order to be able to download the updates (Figure 1.6).

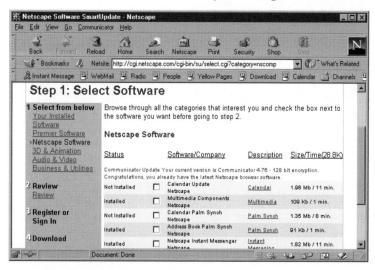

Figure 1.6: Netscape Smart Update

The most up-to-date Netscape browser is Netscape 6, and the current version is 6.01. As already mentioned, this browser is not completely stable, but is widely used, so it is vital that you test your pages in this browser. At present you can download the browser in various languages and for various operating systems (Windows, Linux, Macintosh) from `http://home.netscape.com/uk/download/download_n6.html` The link for "slow connections" only loads a small installation program (similar to Internet Explorer) which in turn downloads individual components from the Internet during the installation. The link for fast connections transfers the complete package to your computer.

There are also several methods of installation (see Figure 1.7), but we recommend CUSTOM, because you should decide whether you want to install the mail program as well as Java support.

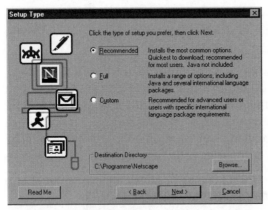

Figure 1.7: Installation methods in Netscape 6

Following the installation, this version also offers the option of automatic updates. You find these in the Windows Start menu under the menu item NETSCAPE SMARTUPDATE (see Figure 1.8) or under the URL `http://home.netscape.com/smartupdate/su1_ie.html`.

Figure 1.8: Netscape SmartUpdate

Opera

The Norwegian browser Opera (Figure 1.9) is regarded as being very fast and this is not only due to its low file size. The construction of its pages is also very fast. For a long time, Opera was costly, but has recently become available free of charge. It was fully financed through an advertising banner which was slotted in and displayed whilst the Web was being surfed. Unfortunately Opera is only number 3 in the browser market, behind Internet Explorer and Netscape Navigator. The plug-in support is not yet fully matured, and pages which look good in Netscape Navigator and Internet Explorer do not automatically look good in Opera. The development of Web sites for two different browsers is already expensive, so lots of agencies, including professionals, struggle to support a third browser, never mind one with a small market share.

If you want to distinguish them from each other, test your pages on Opera. The browser is quickly downloaded (`http://www.opera.com/download/`), the current version is 5.02. The browser is available for Windows, Apple Macintosh and exotic operating systems like Linux BeOS and EPOC.

The installation is carried out here, and also led by the menu, and you don't have to decide which components you wish to install. Before the download, however, you have to choose whether you want to load a version without Java support or to have Java effects and accept a larger download. If you use the browser mainly for testing, it also tests the non-Java variants as well. If you want to surf as well, then you should just use the Java version

Unfortunately, Opera does not support Web-based browser updates. You always have to look at the manufacturer's homepage (`http://www.opera.com`) to see whether a new version is available. As a rule, however, a small update is also available, which only replaces the files which have been changed.

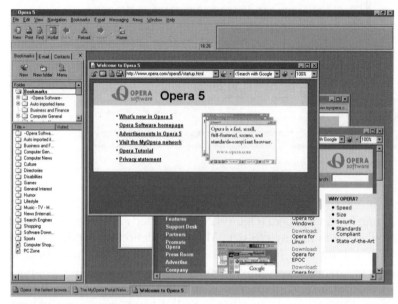

Figure 1.9: Opera in action

Editors

HTML files are pure text files. This means that you can create files with a pure text editor.

Windows

If you use Windows, two editors are supplied at the same time which are found under START/PROGRAM/ACCESSORIES. These two editors are: *Notepad* (or Editor) and *Wordpad*. Both programs are able to save text files, but you must make sure that these files have the endings *htm* or *html* and not *txt*. The process is as follows:

1 Create the HTML pages in Notepad.

2 Choose the menu command FILE/SAVE AS (FIGURE 1.10).

3 Choose the entry ALL FILES (*.*) in the pull-down menu TYPE OF FILE.

4 Give the desired file name with an extension, for example *file.html*. Make sure you enter the file name in inverted commas!

5 Click on SAVE, in order to transfer the file on to your hard drive.

Figure 1.10: The dialogue box SAVE AS

Other operating systems also offer simple editors, for example 'Simpled it' from Apple Macintosh, which work along the same lines.

The functionality of these editors is, however, mostly very basic. For this reason, you should look at alternatives which were better designed for the creation of HTML files.

Notetab

This Windows text editor exists in three variants: Notetab Light is free of charge, while Notetab Standard and Notetab Pro are not free, but offer more functionality. However, Notetab Light (Figure 1.11) is sufficient for most purposes.

You can find all variants under `http://www.notetab.com`. Download one of these and install it. You can now edit HTML files in this editor and make use of a particular function. Important HTML elements can be displayed in a border on the left. With a double-click, these elements are inserted into the open document so you can create HTML files more quickly.

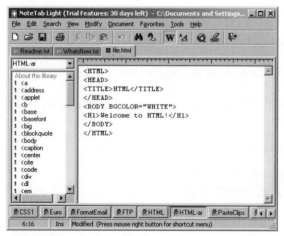

Figure 1.11: NoteTab Light

UltraEdit

UltraEdit (Figure 1.12) is an editor which has more functionality than NoteTab Light, but is not free. Both authors of this book use this. UltraEdit, amongst other things, has a feature called *Syntax Highlighting*. Individual elements of the HTML pages (for example the elements in angled brackets) are shown in another colour, so typing errors can be noticed quicker.

A chronological (but not functional) restricted text version of UltraEdit can be found under `http://www.ultraedit.com`. UltraEdit only runs under Microsoft Windows.

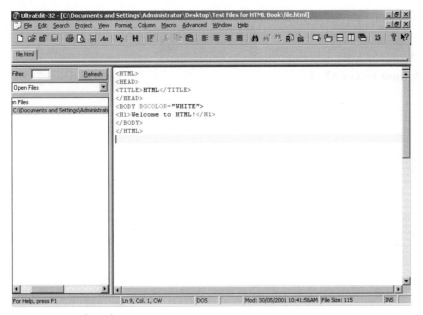

Figure 1.12: UltraEdit

Quick Start

It's about time to get cracking.

1 Create a file `file.html` (as you have already seen in the section What is HTML?, in Figure 1.11 and Figure 1.12) in the editor of your choice.

Here is the code:

```
<HTML>
<HEAD>
<TITLE>HTML</TITLE>
</HEAD>
<BODY BGCOLOR="WHITE">
<H1>Welcome to HTML!</H1>
</BODY>
</HTML>
```

2 Test this file in both Internet Explorer and Netscape (Figure 1.13).

Figure 1.13: The file you have just created, in Netscape Navigator

You now fulfil all the prerequisites to become a successful HTML programmer. In the next chapter we show how to do this.

Chapter 2

HTML – The Basics

*Have you read and followed the introductory chapter?
You are on your way to becoming a real HTML ace
then! In this chapter we lay the foundations. First of
all we create easy HTML pages which you can test in
your browser. You don't have a browser? Then flick
back to Chapter 1 to see how to install one! You don't
have an editor? We also covered this in Chapter 1, so
refer back to this. Otherwise, you are ready for take-off
and can get started!*

The Concepts behind HTML

You already know what HTML is and have even already seen an HTML page (in Chapter 1). There you saw a confusing conglomeration of text and angled brackets (<, >). In the following sections, we will discuss the single components of an HTML page.

Tags

In HTML a tag is written in angled brackets. An example of a tag is `<HTML>`. The use of upper- and lower case is unimportant with HTML-tags, so the following may also be used:

- `<html>`
- `<hTmL>`
- `<HtML>`
- etc.

Within a tag, as many blank characters and empty lines can be used as you like. Only the name of the tag (in the example, HTML) must not be separated. The following variants are therefore possible:

- `<HTML        >`
- `<   HTML   >`
- `<`

  `HTML`

  `>`
- etc.

> **Caution**
>
> *The only exception to this rule is that: no blanks can be used in end-tags (that is </XXX>) as some browsers do not accept this.*

From an author's point of view, these are wonderful conditions because an otherwise damaging radical change in the middle of a long sentence can be avoided – we simply insert changes manually. This way the appearance of the HTML page is not affected.

A tag rarely appears alone. It normally has some kind of content (text, for example). At the end of the content comes an end-tag, which completes this HTML element.

For example, an HTML page begins with the `<HTML>` tag. The actual content of the page follows this, and at the end comes the end-tag, `</HTML>`. The end-tag is written just like the start-tag, only it has a forward slash (/) at the beginning (after the opening angled bracket).

Even when start and end tags are identical (apart from the slash), no distinction is made between upper- and lower case characters. If you begin an HTML element with `<HTML>` you can end it with `</HTML>` or with `</html>` or with `</HtMl>` or ...

The effects the tags have on the contents between them differs from one HTML tag to another. It is not possible to set a rule. Here are three examples:

- `<B>Hello</B>` – leads to **Hello** being output (bold).

- `<I>Hello</I>` – leads to *Hello* being output (italic).

- `<TITLE>Hello</TITLE>` – leads to "Hello" being output as the title of the page.

The first two examples lead to a direct text output and formatting. The third example has effects on the text and in the title of the Web browser. These examples are not as easily combined as one would like them to be. For example, the following is not possible:

```
<TITLE><B>Hello</B></TITLE>
```

The text in the border of the browser cannot be displayed in bold. The following code works in the opposite way to this:

```
<B><I>Hello</I></B>
```

This leads to an output of ***Hello***, which is bold and italic.

Many tags can therefore be used together. You can combine the effects of individual tags, but in doing so you must make sure that the tags are nested correctly:

```
<B><I>Hello</B></I>
```

You must close tags in the reverse order to which you open them. The tag which was opened last will therefore be the first to be closed. The main problem here is Web browsers. They also accept "incorrect" HTML and won't issue an error message when the HTML programmer has done something wrong, but will try to interpret and display the HTML in the best possible way. The term *best possible* is seen here as a purely subjective assessment. Therefore, you should program cleanly so that you don't get any nasty surprises!

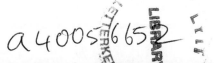

Not every tag has to be closed again. A prime example of this is <HR>. This stands for *horizontal rule*, and represents a horizontal bar in the Web browser (see Figure 2.1). Now think about how a browser should interpret <HR>some text</HR> ; as a label for the horizontal line perhaps? That doesn't make much sense. The creators of HTML also thought this, and for this reason <HR> is an *empty tag*. It also appears only in the form <HR></HR>. There are many tags like this, and you will get to know a large proportion of these in this book!

Figure 2.1: A horizontal rule in the browser (Internet Explorer)

There is also a special variant of a tag which does not obey the usual rules. We are dealing here with comments. Comments are ignored in the display of the HTML page– they speak, but are not shown. So, an HTML programmer can, for example, accommodate copyright notes in the HTML code, and also Information important to the programmer ("The contents start here"). A comment is introduced by <!-- and completed by --> :

```
<!-- Comment to be inserted here! -->
```

Attributes

A tag does not necessarily stand alone. It can also be determined through the output of another parameter nearby. This parameter is called an *attribute*. Attributes are added to a tag as follows:

```
<TAGNAME ATTRIBUTE1="value1" ATTRIBUTE2="value2" ... >
```

For attributes:

- The use of lower- and upper case in attribute names is ignored.

- Blanks and new lines outside the attribute name as well as the value are ignored.

- The order of the attributes does not matter.

- The value of the individual attributes can be contained in quotation marks. Almost all browsers accept the omission of quotation marks, but only *almost* all. You should therefore check this in as many browsers as possible.

- You can only indicate attributes using a start-tag, not with an end-tag.

We come back to our example, the horizontal rules. The <HR> tag recognises the parameter WIDTH, which indicates the width of the bar in pixels (screen points). The following produces three different bar lengths (Figure 2.2).

```
<HR WIDTH="100">
<HR WIDTH="200">
<HR WIDTH="300">
```

Figure 2.2: Three different bar lengths

> **Note**
>
> *Instead of pixel widths you can also state percentage values with which you give the width of the bars in relation to the browser window. For example, <HR WIDTH="50%"> would give a horizontal rule that was half the width of the screen.*

The <HR> tag also knows the parameter SIZE, which gives the thickness of the bar (in pixels). The output of the following code in a browser can be seen in Figure 2.3.

```
<HR SIZE="1">
<HR SIZE="5">
<HR SIZE="10">
```

Figure 2.3: Three different bar thicknesses.

As already mentioned, you can also combine attributes in any order you like. (there is one condition: the tag name must be first). In order to create a bar which is 5 pixels high and 200 pixels wide, use the following HTML code:

```
<HR WIDTH="200" SIZE="5">
```

or

```
<HR SIZE="5" WIDTH="200">
```

Figure 2.4: A bar five pixels high and 200 pixels wide.

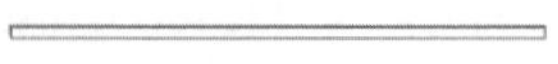

There are also attributes which have no value, similar to tags which have no content. An example of the `<HR>` tag is the attribute `NOSHADE`. Using this, the 3D frame removes itself from around the bar. An attribute without a value is often called a *parameter*, but here we will stick with the more usual label *attribute*.

```
<HR NOSHADE>
```

You can see the result in Figure 2.5; as a comparison, you also see a bar with the 3D shadow.

Figure 2.5: A bar without a 3D frame (above) and one with (below)

Entities

An *entity* is a special character. This is introduced with an ampersand (`&`), then the code for the special character follows, with a semicolon at the end. This can be replaced with ` ` – this stands for *non-breaking space*, or a protected blank character. You will see later, that in HTML, the Web browser automatically carries out the text page proof logically between the individual words. If a non-breaking space comes between two words, there will not be a break at this stage. In Chapter 3 you can find some further examples of entities.

HTML Components

You now know about two most essential concepts in HTML, namely tags and attributes. It's now time for you to start practicing and learn the components of an HTML page. You can make use of the following basic framework:

Basic framework

A (well formed) HTML page always has the following construction:

```
<!-- DOCUMENTTYPE -->
<HTML>
<HEAD>
<!-- Headsection-->
</HEAD>
<BODY>
<!-- contents section -->
</BODY>
</HTML>
```

The tags <HTML>, <HEAD> and <BODY> complete with end-tags are also contained in every HTML document. The head section, enclosed by <HEAD> and </HEAD>, is dealt with in the section titled 'Head Section', and the content section (surrounded by the two tags <BODY> and </BODY>) is dealt with in 'Content Section'.

In the first line, the document type is optional. According to specifications, the HTML sub-version will be indicated here as well as the underlying command sentence. This kind of document can look like this:

```
<!DOCTYPE html PUBLIC "-//W3C//DTD HTML 4.01//EN
    http://www.w3.org/TR/html4/strict.dtd">
```

Admittedly, this is not shown very often, so we'll leave it out here. Web sites are correctly shown in all browsers without this detail. As a rule, an HTML page begins with <HTML> and ends with </HTML>. Everything in between has some kind of effect on what you see in and on the browser.

Head section

The head section is enclosed by <HEAD> and </HEAD>. General information about the HTML page is contained between these; for example, you can put the name of the author or copyright remarks there (more about this in Chapter 11). As well as this, you can give details about how the contents of the HTML file will be formatted for the output in the browser (see Chapter 10). The most frequently used componet in the head section is the <TITLE> element. You can indicate the title of the HTML page in this. Look at the following HTML code:

```
<HTML>
<HEAD>
<TITLE>HTML is really easy to learn!</TITLE>
</HEAD>
<BODY>
<!-- content section -->
</BODY>
</HTML>
```

You see that the title has been shown between `<TITLE>` and `</TITLE>` as pure text. If you load this page in your Web browser at first you will see nothing, because the page has no content. However, you still find the page title in the title strip of your browser, and also the type of browser being used (see Figure 2.6).

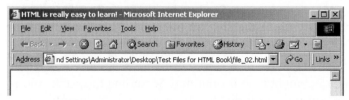

Figure 2.6: The text is inserted into the title strip of the browser

The following rule should help: the details in the head section of an HTML page do not lead to any output in the display area of the browser. You can indicate background information about the HTML page and insert text into the title strip of the browser. The content section is responsible for the output.

You should use the title strip of the browser to add information. If you search for a term using a search engine and receive a hit list, you also get every page title of every hit reported to you. This is exactly what you write between `<TITLE>` and `</TITLE>`. So, use a short but concise title!

Content section

The content section is surrounded by `<BODY>` and `</BODY>`. Everything that is given there will be displayed in the browser window. The tags which you already know, `<B>`, `<I>` and `<HR>` will also be used in the content section. They have no effect in the heading section. Which tags have what effect will be covered in the following ten chapters. First of all we will try out the tags you already know:

```
<HTML>
<HEAD>
<TITLE>HTML is really easy to learn!</TITLE>
</HEAD>
<BODY>
Hello!
<HR>
<B>Hello! (bold)</B>
<HR NOSHADE>
<I>Hello! (italic)</I>
<HR WIDTH="50%" SIZE="5">
<B><I>Hello! (bold and italic)</I></B>
</BODY>
</HTML>
```

The results of the above code are shown in Figure 2.7 below.

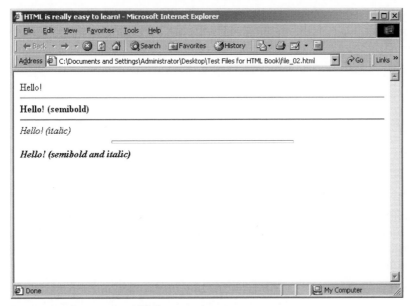

Figure 2.7: Our present HTML repertoire

A first HTML page

We will end this brief introduction by creating your first example page. Generally, when creating a Web page, you proceed as follows :

1 Create a new document in your editor and save it (cf. Chapter 1).

2 Begin with <HTML> and </HTML>.

3 Then create the head section: <HEAD> and </HEAD>.

4 Give a page title within the head section between <TITLE> and </TITLE>.

5 Now create the content section <BODY> and </BODY> between </HEAD> and </HTML> .

6 Give the content of the page within the content section: text, bars, etc. You will learn what your options are in the next chapter!

7 Save the updated document when you have finished, but also save it regularly in between as well: *save early, save often.*

Now we will create our first HTML page and see how text will be displayed in the browser. First of all, create an HTML core according to the following pattern:

```
<HTML>
<HEAD>
<TITLE>Goethe</TITLE>
</HEAD>
<BODY>
</BODY>
</HTML>
```

You see that we have chosen "Goethe" as the page title and want to use a familiar quotation in the contents area. In *Wilhelm Meister's Years of Travel* we have struck lucky, the following passage is about the arranging of leisure time and hypochonertum:

> *Man is a limited being. Sundays are devoted to reconsidering our restrictions. It is material sufferings that we barely notice during the frenzy of the week, so we immediately have to consult the doctor. If our restrictions are economic and even civic, so our professionals are*

required to observe their agenda. If that which plagues us is intellectual or moral, so we have a friend, a confidante to whom to turn, and whose advice and influence to seek: enough, that is the law: nobody may prolong a worry or grievance into the new week.

We now take this text and place it in the content area of the HTML page. For technical reasons we insert blank lines in our text in order to keep the book looking clear and simple:

```
<HTML>

<HEAD>

<TITLE>Goethe</TITLE>

</HEAD>

<BODY>

Man is a limited being. Sundays are devoted

to reconsidering our restrictions. It is material

sufferings that we barely notice during the frenzy

of the week, so we immediately consult the doctor,

If our restrictions are economic and even civic, so our

professionals are required to observe their agenda.

If that which plagues us is intellectual or moral, so

we have a friend, a confidante to whom to turn, and whose

advice and influence to seek: enough, that is the law:

nobody may prolong a worry or grievance into the new week.

</BODY>

</HTML>
```

How do you think this HTML document will be shown in your browser? Is the text broken in the places in which we have broken the text here? The answer to this question can be seen in Figure 2.8.

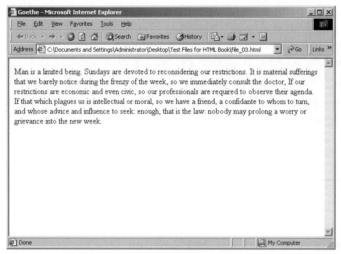
Figure 2.8: The text in the browser with automatic line breaks

As you can see, the browser has completely ignored our hard line breaks. Instead, it has chosen line breaks at the end of the page. You can easily check this yourself if you change the size of the browser window. No scrollbars appear, but the text is simply broken up so that lines are shorter (Figure 2.9).

Figure 2.9: The same text viewed in a smaller browser window

As you can see, in HTML, line breaks make no difference to how your page is displayed. This is an advantage for you as you can lay out your code clearly with lots of line breaks, and short lines, so you can see what you have done.

However, we want to look in more detail at the effects of line breaks. In the following, you find a modified version of the above listing, only this time the line breaks are in the middle of words:

```
<HTML>
<HEAD>
<TITLE>Goethe</TITLE>
</HEAD>
<BODY>
<BODY>
Man is a limited being. Sundays are devoted
to reconsidering our restrictions. It is mat
erial  sufferings that we barely notice duri
ng the frenzy of the week, so we immediately
consult the doctor, If our restrictions are
economic and even civic, so our  professiona
ls are required to observe their agenda. If
that which plagues us is intellectual or mor
al, so we have a friend, a confidante to whom
to turn, and whose advice and influence to se
ek: enough, that is the law: nobody may prolo
ng a worry or grievance into the new week.
</BODY>
</HTML>
```

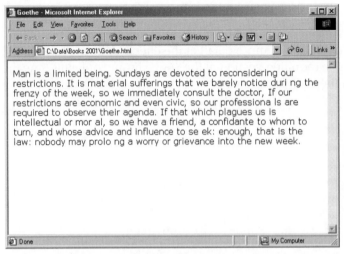

Figure 2.10: blanks came from line skips

As you can see from Figure 2.10, the browser has provided for the line breaks itself. However, our manual line breaks led to blank spaces (see the second line, mat erial) The reason is as follows: a Web browser combines a row of characters under the generic term *whitespace*. This includes:

- Blank spaces
- Line breaks
- Tabs

In the description, a character such as this will be dealt with like a blank space. Now you ask yourself, why then, in the previous examples, was the gap between the individual words not bigger? This question can also be answered directly with a glance at the browser. Take a look at the following HTML document:

```
<HTML>
<HEAD>
<TITLE>Goethe</TITLE>
</HEAD>
<BODY>
```

```
Johann    Wolfgang    von




Goethe
</BODY>
</HTML>
```

Here, you see three blank spaces between "Johann" and "Wolfgang" and between "Wolfgang" and "von", as well as six blank lines between "von" and "Goethe". Type out the example above and take a look at Figure 2.11!

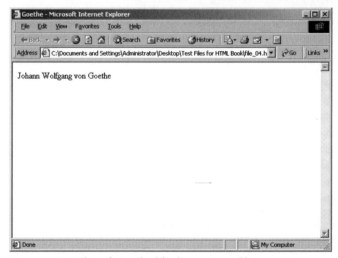

Figure 2.11: Where have the blank spaces and lines gone?

As you can see, the gaps between the individual words are the same and are about as big as a normal space but not as big as three. This is because several whitespace characters following one another are blended together to form one single blank for the display. It doesn't matter whether you use one, five, or ten blank spaces between words, the result is the same. To increase the gaps between words, you must use other tricks. An example of this is the entity which was introduced in the section 'Entities': , which represents a non-breaking space. You can put several of these behind one another, or can combine them with blank spaces. The following code actually leaves three blank spaces respectively between the individual name components (blank space-non-breaking space-blank space)(Figure 2.12).

```
<HTML>

<HEAD>

<TITLE>Goethe</TITLE>

</HEAD>

<BODY>

Johann   Wolfgang   von   Goethe

</BODY>

</HTML>
```

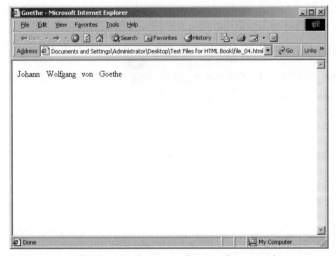

Figure 2.12: The distance between the words is now bigger

We end the chapter on this point. You have now learnt the basic construction of HTML and have created your first HTML page. In the next chapter we want to build on this knowledge and discuss text output as well as the formatting options.

Chapter 3

Text

In the beginning there was the Word. And in this book we also want to begin with the word, or rather text. In this chapter you see how you can display text on HTML pages, which formatting options there are for text (typeface and size), and the options available for text alignment. Note: from this chapter onwards, we will only indicate the contents of the HTML page because the base code for all HTML pages is the same, and this space can be better filled.

Text output

As you saw in Chapter 2, text output is easy in HTML. The browser automatically processes the page proof and you are only responsible for the actual production of the text.

Admittedly this is a slight exaggeration. You can of course intervene, particularly in the breaks.

Breaks between paragraphs

If you want to program completely accurate HTML, and let's assume you do, you have to order your text into paragraphs. Text does not hang around freely in the content section of the HTML page, but is always within a paragraph. Therefore, a paragraph is labelled with the HTML tag <P>. In the following HTML code there are two paragraphs (Figure 3.1):

```
<P>

<BODY>

Man is a limited being. Sundays are devoted

to reconsidering our restrictions. It is material

sufferings that we barely notice during the frenzy

of the week, so we immediately consult the doctor,

If our restrictions are economic and even civic, so our

professionals are required to observe their agenda.

If that which plagues us is intellectual or moral, so

we have a friend, a confidante to whom to turn, and whose

advice and influence to seek: enough, that is the law:

nobody may prolong a worry or grievance into the new week.

</P>

<P>

From: Johann Wolfgang von Goethe,

Wilhelm Meister's Years of Travel

</P>
```

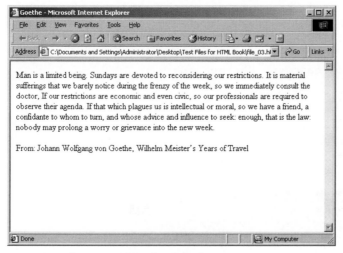

Figure 3.1: The two paragraphs in the browser

From this you can gather that starting a new paragraph puts a line space after the first paragraph. This gap is relatively big. You can call this a paragraph gap. If you want to produce normal line spacing (the gap between the two lines in flowing text) you need to use the <BR> tag. Here, BR stands for *line break*.

A line break <BR> does not end a paragraph. You should therefore always put the tag within a paragraph. In practice, two line breaks <BR> produce a gap, which you would keep when changing a paragraph. You can treat it as a rule: small gaps <BR>, big gaps also <BR> and with paragraph gaps always <P>.

```
<P>

<BODY>

Man is a limited being. Sundays are devoted
to reconsidering our restrictions. It is material
sufferings that we barely notice during the frenzy
of the week, so we immediately consult the doctor.
If our restrictions are economic and even civic, so our
professionals are required to observe their agenda.
If that which plagues us is intellectual or moral, so
we have a friend, a confidante to whom to turn, and whose
advice and influence to seek: enough, that is the law:
```

35

```
nobody may prolong a worry or grievance into the new week.

<BR>

<BR>

From: Johann Wolfgang von Goethe, <BR>

Wilhelm Meister's Years of Travel

</P>

<P>

A recommended book!

</P>
```

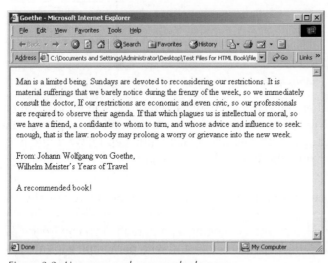

Figure 3.2: Line gaps and paragraph changes

Look at Figure 3.2: between the Goethe extract and the recommendation, there are two line breaks and a paragraph change. In the middle of the quote another line change is hidden.

Normally the text breaks itself up automatically, and the browser searches for a blank (a break in the middle of a word is not found as a rule). You can prevent this kind of break with the non-breaking space already mentioned: .

If you want to protect the whole area of the text from breaks you can use the <NOBR> tag. NOBR stands for *no break* and works in the following way:

```
<P>

<NOBR>

<BODY>
```

```
Man is a limited being. Sundays are devoted
to reconsidering our restrictions. </NOBR> It is material
sufferings that we barely notice during the frenzy
of the week, so we immediately consult the doctor.
</P>
```

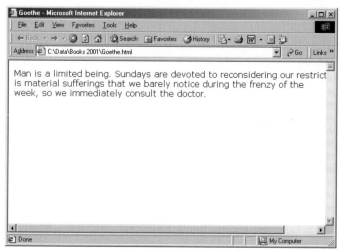

Figure 3.3: The line break has been prevented.

As you can see from Figure 3.3, the first sentence is not broken up. This is why there is a horizontal scrollbar. The next sentence is, in turn, broken up automatically on the right hand edge of the browser, and is then no longer found within the <NOBR> element.

The reasons for doing this are mostly visual. Imagine that you want to create a price list for your products on line. There should be no break between the price and the currency, as this would not look good. Therefore, you should use the code according to the following pattern:

```
<P>Nur 99,99 EUR.</P>
```

In longer text passages, <NOBR> can be used.

Text alignment

By default, the text is always justified to the left, like the text in this book. Using the ALIGN attribute of the <P> tag you can align the text elsewhere. The following values are available:

- LEFT – The default, left-justified.
- CENTER – The paragraph is centred.
- RIGHT – Right-alignment.
- JUSTIFY – Justification is not, however, supported by all browsers.

The following listing uses all three options (Figure 3.4):

```
<P ALIGN="LEFT">
Man is a limited being. Sundays are devoted
to reconsidering our restrictions.
</P>
<P ALIGN="CENTER">
It is the material sufferings that we barely
notice during the frenzy of the week, so we
immediately consult the doctor.
</P>
<P ALIGN="RIGHT">
If our restrictions are economic and even civic,
so our professionals are required to observe
their agenda.
</P>
<P ALIGN="JUSTIFY">
If that which plagues us is intellectual or moral,
so we have a friend, a confidante to whom to turn
and whose advice and influence to seek: enough,
that is the law: nobody may prolong a worry or
grievance into the new week</P>
```

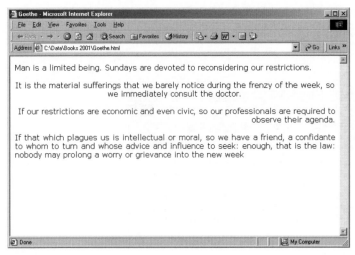

Figure 3.4: Left, right, and centre alignment and justification

You can see the result in Figure 3.4: The four paragraphs are aligned to the left, the centre, right, and justified.

If you want to align several elements as paragraphs, (examples of these elements can be found below as well as in the following chapter), you can use <DIV> instead of <P>. The effect of <DIV> is comparable to <P> with the difference that <P> is only allowed to contain text, but no headings, for example. From the attributes, the tag knows ALIGN with the possible values LEFT, RIGHT and CENTER. JUSTIFY is missing because only text can be justified.

```
<DIV ALIGN="LEFT">

Man is a limited being. Sundays are devoted

to reconsidering our restrictions.

</DIV>

<DIV ALIGN="CENTER">

If our restrictions are economic and even civic,

so our professionals are required to observe

their agenda.

</DIV>

<DIV ALIGN="RIGHT">

If that which plagues us is intellectual or moral,

so we have a friend, a confidante to whom to turn
```

```
and whose advice and influence to seek: enough,
that is the law: nobody may prolong a worry or
grievance into the new week</P>
</DIV>
```

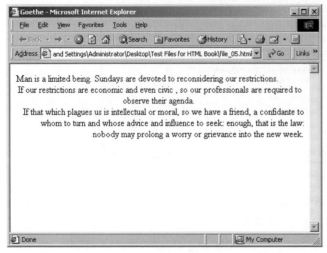

Figure 3.5: This time this is carried out using `<DIV>`.

In Figure 3.5 you can see the difference straight away: the large gap between the paragraphs has gone; however, the alignments and the breaks have taken their place.

Earlier, when `<DIV>` did not exist, Web designers used the tag `<CENTER>`, which could centre HTML elements. This element has now become obsolete and should no longer be used.

Formatting text

Now that you already know (almost) all of the ways to produce text, we will now move on to the text formatting. In HTML, a choice has to be made between *logical* and *physical* formatting. In logical formatting, tags are used to express what you are aiming at with the formatting. The formatting is taken on by the browser itself. An example is the tag `<STRONG>`. Through this, a text becomes strongly emphasised:

```
<P>
Man is a <STRONG> limited
```

```
being</STRONG>. Sundays are <STRONG>devoted
</STRONG> to reconsidering our restrictions.
</P>
```

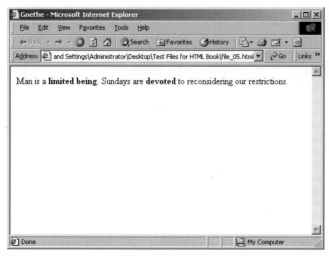

Figure 3.6: The emphasised text is displayed in bold

As you can gather from Figure 3.6, the browser displays the marked text in bold, but this is left to the browser to do this itself. Other browsers may for example, display the text in italics, or not at all. Because the appearance of Web sites is usually important, you cannot afford to leave interpretation to the browser. For this reason there are tags which provide for physical text formatting, whose effects are defined from here onwards. We will concentrate on this method of formatting because it simply does more. We will begin with logical formatting.

Headings

There are six heading levels available. These are numbered from 1 to 6, with 1 being the biggest heading and 6 the smallest. You can subdivide the text with these, but otherwise they have no influence on appearance and text size (you will learn this in Chapter 9). The headings produce new paragraphs, but must be used outside a <P> element, rather than within. The individual tags are:

- <H1> – Heading 1.

- `<H2>` – Heading 2.
- `<H3>` – Heading 3.
- `<H4>` – Heading 4.
- `<H5>` – Heading 5.
- `<H6>` – Heading 6.
- The following listing represents all of the font types. Notice how the normal text behaves in relation to the headings (Figure 3.7)!

```
<H1>heading level 1.</H1>
<H2>heading level 2.</H2>
<H3>heading level 3.</H3>
<H4>heading level 4.</H4>
<H5>heading level 5.</H5>
<H6>heading level 6.</H6>
<P>normal text</P>
```

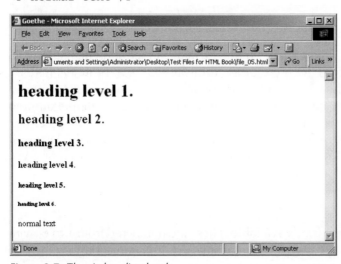

Figure 3.7: The six heading levels

You can align headings in the same way as you can paragraphs. The appropriate attribute is called ALIGN with the possible values LEFT, CENTER and RIGHT (The attribute JUSTIFY, from when we were dealing with paragraphs, is not yet supported by a browser).

```
<H1 ALIGN="LEFT">heading aligned left</H1>
```

```
<H1 ALIGN="CENTER">heading centred</H1>
<H1 ALIGN="RIGHT">heading aligned right</H1>
```

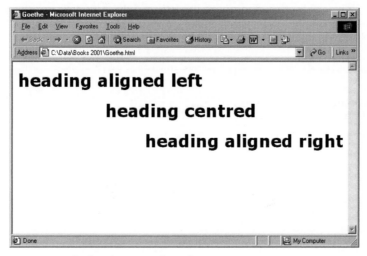

Figure 3.8: The headings are aligned

Character formats

We introduced one of the possible character formats to you in Chapter 2 – do you remember the italic and bold characters? Now we will show you some more of these. You can use these marks on any text element that you like, but be careful: you should only use the tag within a paragraph, not outside it.

Here is an overview of the different kinds of font formatting available in HTML, in alphabetical order:

- `<B>` – Text is displayed in bold
- `<BIG>` – Text is displayed bigger
- `<BLINK>` – Text is displayed flashing (Netscape only)
- `<I>` – Text is displayed in italics
- `<SMALL>` – Text is displayed smaller
- `<STRIKE>` – Text is displayed as strike-through
- `<SUB>` – Text is placed lower
- `<SUP>` – Text is placed higher
- `<TT>` – Text is displayed in a monospaced font (such as Courier)

- <U> – Text is displayed as underlined

The following listing uses all of these options once, and many are also used in combination with each other. Compare the listing with the corresponding screenshot (Figure 3.9)!

```
<P>

Man is a <B>limited</B> being. <BIG>Sundays</BIG> are
devoted

to reconsidering our <BIG>restrictions</BIG>. It is
<BLINK>material

sufferings<BLINK> that we <SMALL>barely</SMALL> notice dur-
ing the frenzy

of the week, so we <STRIKE>immediately</STRIKE> consult the
doctor,

If our <B><SMALL>restrictions</SMALL></B> are economic and
even<SUB>civic</SUB>, so our professionals are required to
observe their<SUP>agenda</SUP>.

If that which plagues us is intellectual or moral, so

we have a friend, a confidante to whom to turn, and whose

advice and influence to seek: <TT>enough, that is the law:

nobody may prolong a worry or grievance into the new week.</
TT>

</P>
```

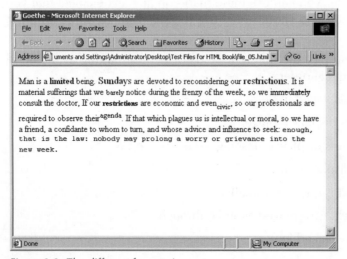

Figure 3.9: The different formats in use

The tags which are used most often are <B> and <I>. Bold and italic type are popular forms of layout and, when used sparingly, can enormously improve the appearance of a Web site. As an example, see the cutting from the US magazine Newsweek Online (www.newsweek.com) in Figure 3.10 which uses bold and italic type.

Figure 3.10: The Newsweek site uses (amongst other things) italic and bold

The next most frequently used tags for formatting are <BIG> and <SMALL>, which make text larger or smaller. However, their use is not optimal because you cannot state by how much the text will grow larger or smaller. In the section on 'fonts' you will learn how you can control this more precisely. However, it is worthwhile, in any case, to look at the difference to get a feel for how much larger or smaller the text will be.:

```
<P>
   <SMALL>Goethe</SMALL>
   Goethe
   <BIG>Goethe</BIG>
</P>
```

Figure 3.11: The text in small, normal, and large

Subscript and superscript text, for example, appears in mathematic formulae:

```
<P>
    c<SUB>1</SUB><SUP>2</SUP> +
    c<SUB>2</SUB><SUP>2</SUP>=
    c<SUB>3</SUB><SUP>2</SUP>
</P>
```

These characters are not, however, made smaller, so you should use the `<sub>` or `<sup>` tag with `<SMALL>` (Figure 3.12):

```
<P>
    c<SUB><SMALL>1</SMALL></SUB>
    <SUP><SMALL>2</SMALL></SUP> +
    c<SUB><SMALL>2</SMALL></SUB>
    <SUP><SMALL>2</SMALL></SUP> =
    c<SUB><SMALL>3</SMALL></SUB>
    <SUP><SMALL>2</SMALL></SUP>
</P>
```

Figure 3.12: Exponents and indices

In Figure 3.12 you can see the difference: the top equation uses a normal font size, while the lower one uses a smaller font.

However, you can also imitate footnotes with <SUP>. Simply place a superscript number (or a sign) where you want it in the text and fix a horizontal bar at the end of the text (see Chapter 1), and then the footnote (Figure 3.13). In Chapter 4, you will learn how you can scroll to the footnote by clicking on it.

```
<P>
Man is a limited being. Sundays <SUP>1</SUP> are devoted
to reconsidering our restrictions. It is material
sufferings that we barely notice during the frenzy
of the week, so we immediately consult the doctor.
If our restrictions are economic and even civic, so our
professionals are required to observe their agenda.
If that which plagues us is intellectual or moral, so
we have a friend, a confidante to whom to turn, and whose
advice and influence to seek: enough, that is the law:
nobody may prolong a worry or grievance into the new
week.<SUP>2</SUP>
</P>
<HR>
<P>
<SUP>1</SUP>Seventh day of the week<BR>
<SUP>2</SUP>From: Wilhelm Meister's Years of Travel
</P>
```

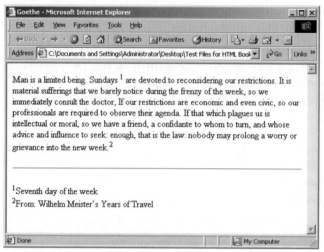

Man is a limited being. Sundays [1] are devoted to reconsidering our restrictions. It is material sufferings that we barely notice during the frenzy of the week, so we immediately consult the doctor. If our restrictions are economic and even civic, so our professionals are required to observe their agenda. If that which plagues us is intellectual or moral, so we have a friend, a confidante to whom to turn, and whose advice and influence to seek: enough, that is the law: nobody may prolong a worry or grievance into the new week. [2]

[1] Seventh day of the week.
[2] From: Wilhelm Meister's Years of Travel

Figure 3.13: Footnotes are added to the text

To end this section we want to give another two warnings. The first concerns the `<U>` -tag. With this, you can display text as underlined. On the World Wide Web, however, text for links is underlined; you can read more about this in Chapter 4. For this reason you should avoid using this tag.

The second warning concerns the `<BLINK>` tag. An informal rule says: The more unprofessional the page, the more often this tag is used. The tag functions exclusively on Netscape Navigator and the flashing only irritates most visitors. Good contents rather than graphic effects should make your pages more eye-catching!

At this point we should also mention a "nasty" tag. It is called `<MARQUEE>` and produces moving text. Netscape Navigator does not support this tag, so you should refrain from using it.

Fonts

If you take another look back at Figure 3.10 you will see that the font used there is obviously Arial, not Times New Roman, which is the default of a Web browser. You may have already guessed that you can also change the document type, font size, and font colour in HTML.

The central tag for this is `<FONT>`. This has many attributes, with which you can decide on the appearance of the text.

Typeface

We will begin with the typeface. You can indicate the name of the typeface here. If this document type is installed on the user's system, the document is shown in this typeface. Otherwise, the default typeface or the most similar typeface possible is used. The appropriate attribute of the `<FONT>` tag is called `FACE`:

```
<P>
<FONT FACE="Times News Roman">Times New
     Roman</FONT><BR>
<FONT FACE="Arial">Arial</FONT><BR>
<FONT FACE="Verdana">Verdana</FONT><BR>
<FONT FACE="Tahoma">Tahoma</FONT><BR>
<FONT FACE="Comic Sans MS">Comic Sans
     MS</FONT><BR>
<FONT FACE="Pearson">Pearson</FONT>
</P>
```

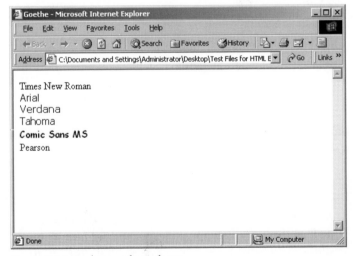

Figure 3.14: A choice of typefaces

In Figure 3.14 you can see what happens if a typeface is given which is not installed on the user's system (in our case this was the fantasy typeface "Pearson"): It will use the default typeface, in this case, Times New Roman. Do not rely on Times New Roman being the default, as users can change this individually in their browser options.

The fonts used up to now are almost entirely exclusive to Windows. These fonts are also available under Unix/Linux and Macintosh, (or at least are very similar), but some of them have different names. For example, Arial is known as Helvetica in different operating systems, and Geneva is very similar, and Times New Roman is sometimes called Times elsewhere. You can now give a list of alternative fonts as values of FACE attributes, separated by commas. The browser tries out these fonts one after the other and uses them if it finds one of the fonts in the system (Figure 3.15):

```
<P>
<FONT FACE="Arial,Helvetica,Geneva">
this text almost always appears in Arial.
</FONT><BR>
<FONT FACE="Times New Roman,Times">
and this in Times New Roman.
</FONT>
</P>
```

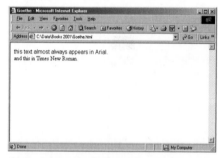

Figure 3.15: The best solution: several typefaces

Font size

In HTML there are seven font sizes, numbered from 1 to 7. We are dealing here with *relative* font sizes, which orientate themselves in the default font size in the Web browser. Here are the various sizes:

- 1 – smallest size, about 8 points (pts) compared with the default size of 12 pts
- 2 – second smallest size, about 10 pts
- 3 – default size, as a rule, 12 pts
- 4 – 14 pts
- 5 – 18 pts
- 6 – 24 pts
- 7 – 36 pts

Most browsers are configured with a default font size of 12 pts, and you can use these values as clues to the point sizes of the other font sizes.

There are two options for inputting font size, and both involve the SIZE attribute of the <FONT> tag. You can either indicate the font size directly, as follows (Figure 3.16):

```
<P>
<FONT SIZE="1">Size 1</FONT><BR>
<FONT SIZE="2">Size 2</FONT><BR>
<FONT SIZE="3">Size 3</FONT><BR>
<FONT SIZE="4">Size 4</FONT><BR>
<FONT SIZE="5">Size 5</FONT><BR>
<FONT SIZE="6">Size 6</FONT><BR>
<FONT SIZE="7">Size 7</FONT>
</P>
```

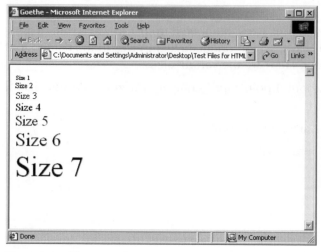

Figure 3.16: The seven font sizes

Or you can indicate the font size as a "normal" font size. With `SIZE="+2"` you make the text two sizes larger than before, while with `SIZE="-3"` you make it three sizes smaller (Figure 3.17):

```
<P>

<FONT SIZE="3">This is size 3.<BR>

<FONT SIZE="+2">And this is size 5.<BR>

<FONT SIZE="-3">And this is size 2.<BR>

</FONT></FONT></FONT>

</P>
```

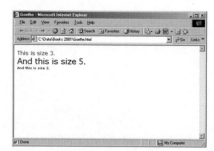

Figure 3.17: Relative font sizes

In order to try out the relative font sizes, temporarily increase the font size in your browser. In Internet Explorer choose VIEW/TEXT SIZE/LARGEST; in

Netscape Navigator put in a high value in the pull-down menu EDIT/PREFERENCES/APPEARANCE/FONTS.

Figure 3.18: The same example in the larger standard font

Font colour

Colour values can be indicated in two ways in HTML: either using their names or using their RGB codes. Screen colours are mixed from the three additive base colours: red, green, and blue (in contrast to the subtractive base colours yellow, red and blue which we know from school). In HTML, you have to indicate how many components of red, green and blue are contained in a colour, and also indicate this as a number between 0 and 255. For example, 255 red components, 0 green components and 0 blue components produce a rich, pure red, whereas 255 red components, 255 green components and 0 blue components produce yellow. 255 red components, 255 green components and 255 blue components produce white and 0 components from every base colour produce black.

You must now convert these proportions to hexadecimal values. Here is a small digression to this:

In the decimal system there are ten numbers from 0 to 9. In the hexadecimal system there are 16 figures: 0 to 9 and then A to F. The "figure" F has also the value of 15. If you now have a two-digit figure, for example FF, you have to multiply the first figure by 16 and add two figures to this in order to get the value. For FF, this is: 15 * 16 + 15 = 255.

Now back to the colours: in order to generate a colour code you have to change the proportions for red, green and blue into two-digit hexadecimal numbers, add them to one another, and put a double hash sign (#) at the front. Yellow has the colour code #FF0000 (255 red components, 0 components from the other two colours), yellow has the colour code #FFFF00, white has #FFFFFF and black has #000000.

If this is too complicated for you, you can also select an abbreviation and use a colour name which has already been defined. The following table shows an overview of all colour names in HTML as well as their corresponding colour codes. In this, we use the "old" specification HTML 3.2, as the current version 4.01 is not entirely supported by all browsers with regards to the colour names.

Colour name	Colour code
Black	#000000
Silver	#C0C0C0
Grey	#808080
White	#FFFFFF
Maroon	#800000
Red	#FF0000
Purple	#800080
Fuchsia	#FF00FF
Green	#008000
Lime	#00FF00
Olive	#808000
Yellow	#FFFF00
Navy	#000080
Blue	#0000FF
Teal	#008080
Aqua	#00FFFF

Table 3.1: The basic colours in HTML

It makes no difference whether you use a colour name or a colour code; you must still use this value in the COLOR attribute of the <FONT> tag in order to make text different colours. Of course, you can also mix the COLOR attribute with the attributes FACE and SIZE.

The following HTML code shows all of the 16 colours; in Figure 3.19 these are shown in the browser, but some are very faint or cannot be seen clearly because of the background colour.

```
<P>
<FONT COLOR="Black">Black</FONT><BR>
<FONT COLOR="Silver">Silver</FONT><BR>
<FONT COLOR="Grey">Grey</FONT><BR>
<FONT COLOR="White">White</FONT><BR>
<FONT COLOR="Maroon">Maroon</FONT><BR>
<FONT COLOR="Red">Red</FONT><BR>
<FONT COLOR="Purple">Purple</FONT><BR>
<FONT COLOR="Fuchsia">Fuchsia</FONT><BR>
<FONT COLOR="Green">Green</FONT><BR>
<FONT COLOR="Lime">Lime</FONT><BR>
<FONT COLOR="Olive">Olive</FONT><BR>
<FONT COLOR="Yellow">Yellow</FONT><BR>
<FONT COLOR="Navy">Navy</FONT><BR>
<FONT COLOR="Blue">Blue</FONT><BR>
<FONT COLOR="Teal">Teal</FONT><BR>
<FONT COLOR="Aqua">Aqua</FONT><BR>
</P>
```

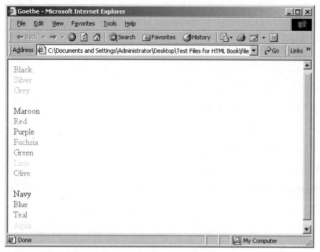

Figure 3.19: The 16 basic colours

To end this chapter there is yet another note: You can also use these colour codes in other places, which you will learn about in Chapter 4. At this point, here is another tip as to how you can indicate the background colour of the HTML page. For this you require the corresponding colour code, and you must give this as a value in the BGCOLOR attribute of the <BODY> tag. In the example above, you can see that not all text is visible because the background is white. For this reason we will take a really bright colour (#EEEEEE) as the background colour, so that all of the text is visible (Figure 3.20).

```
<HTML>
<HEAD>
<TITLE>The 16 basic colours</TITLE>
</HEAD>
<BODY BGCOLOR="#EEEEEE">
<P>
<FONT COLOR="Black">Black</FONT><BR>
<FONT COLOR="Silver">Silver</FONT><BR>
<FONT COLOR="Grey">Grey</FONT><BR>
<FONT COLOR="White">White</FONT><BR>
<FONT COLOR="Maroon">Maroon</FONT><BR>
```

```
<FONT COLOR="Red">Red</FONT><BR>
<FONT COLOR="Purple">Purple</FONT><BR>
<FONT COLOR="Fuchsia">Fuchsia</FONT><BR>
<FONT COLOR="Green">Green</FONT><BR>
<FONT COLOR="Lime">Lime</FONT><BR>
<FONT COLOR="Olive">Olive</FONT><BR>
<FONT COLOR="Yellow">Yellow</FONT><BR>
<FONT COLOR="Navy">Navy</FONT><BR>
<FONT COLOR="Blue">Blue</FONT><BR>
<FONT COLOR="Teal">Teal</FONT><BR>
<FONT COLOR="Aqua">Aqua</FONT><BR>
</P>
</BODY>
</HTML>
```

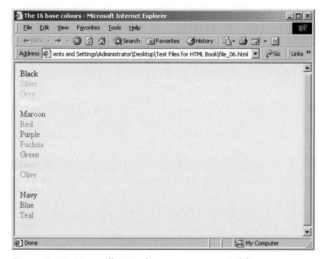

Figure 3.20: Now all 16 colour names are visible

The background colour can also be adjusted by the user in his Web browser. In Internet Explorer this is white as default, while in Netscape Navigator it is almost always grey. So, if you surf the World Wide Web and find a page with an unsuitable grey background, the designer has only tested his pages in Internet Explorer. This is a bad mistake, and one that is very easy to avoid. Simply use `<BODY BGCOLOR="White">` or `<BODY BGCOLOR="#FFFFFF">` to make the background white.

Chapter 4

Lists

This book consists of many numbered lists. We'll let you into a secret: in these lists we have not numbered the lists by hand, and have not laboriously indented paragraphs manually either – our page layout software has done it all itself (almost). If you want to create HTML pages and number them consecutively you also have the choice of doing it all by hand or letting the browser do all the work. Choose the latter; you will learn everything you need to know in this chapter.

Unnumbered lists

Assume that you are working on a presentation and want to arrange some of your arguments into some main points. Admittedly, for this purpose you can use presentation software like Microsoft Powerpoint, for example, but HTML has the advantage that it is platform independent, and is found on almost every computer which has had a Web browser installed – and that is most of them.

Creating lists

We will now turn to how to make such a list. Proceed as follows:

1 First create a HTML page.

2 Begin with a list in the body <BODY> section with the tag <UL> – this stands for unnumbered list.

3 Now create the first element of the list and surround it with <LI> and </LI>. this stands for *list item*.

4 Repeat Step 3 several times and add more elements to the list.

5 When you have finished, end the list with </UL>.

After you have carried out these steps, you will see a code in your editor according to the following pattern (we have left out the HTML basic code for once):

```
<UL>
  <LI>
    Apple
  </LI>
  <LI>
    Pear
  </LI>
  <LI>
    Orange
  </LI>
</UL>
```

Figure 4.1 shows how the browser looks then.

Figure 4.1: Your unnumbered list in the browser

You can format list elements, for example change colours and typefaces, or introduce breaks. This is one of the biggest advantages of an unnumbered list, because every element is indented. You can see this best in an example. In the following code there are two unnumbered points, the first contains a long text, and the second contains some line breaks.

```
<UL>
  <LI>
    Man is a limited being. Sundays are devoted
to reconsidering our restrictions. It is material
sufferings that we barely notice during the frenzy
of the week, so we immediately consult the doctor.
  </LI>
  <LI>
    this text is an excerpt from<br>
     <I>Wilhelm Meister's Years of Travel</I><BR>
    from Goethe.
  </LI>
</UL>
```

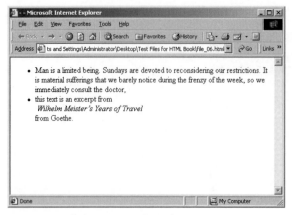

Figure 4.2: All the text is indented

Looking at Figure 4.2 you should notice the following:

- The longer text breaks itself up automatically on the right edge of the displayed area: the next line is indented correspondingly.

- The text with the manual line breaks is broken up at the places which have been indicated, and the next lines are also indented.

You can therefore see that you no longer have to bother formatting the breaks. In addition to this, the resolution and the size of the user's browser window does not matter because the browser calculates it all for you. Of course, you can obtain the same effect with 'hard' (manual) breaks and lots of blank spaces (or) but doing it this way, all your lines have a fixed length.

Changing symbols

As you can see, the browser uses a small circle as an enumeration symbol. This is the same with all current browsers. There are, however, several options available. In HTML there are three types of symbols:

- CIRCLE
- DISC
- SQUARE

You can indicate these values as a TYPE attribute of the <UL> tag. The following code uses all these symbols as an example:

```
<UL TYPE="CIRCLE">
  <LI>
    Apple
  </LI>
  <LI>
    Pear
  </LI>
  <LI>
    Orange
  </LI>
</UL>
<UL TYPE="DISC">
  <LI>
    Potato
  </LI>
  <LI>
    Salad
  </LI>
  <LI>
    Onion
  </LI>
</UL>
<UL TYPE="SQUARE">
<LI>
    Ketchup
  </LI>
  <LI>
    Mayonnaise
  </LI>
  <LI>
    Mustard
  </LI>
</UL>
```

Netscape Navigator (seen in Figure 4.3) shows the whole more or less as expected, but Internet Explorer appears to ignore the instructions and only displays circular symbols (Figure 4.4).

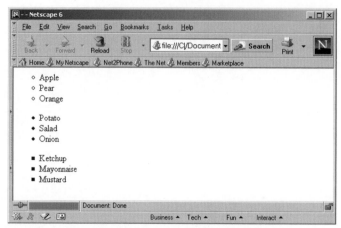

Figure 4.3: Netscape Navigator: all symbols are there

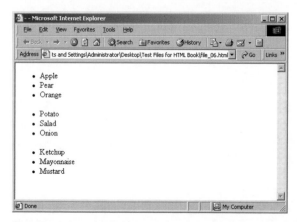

Figure 4.4: Internet Explorer: where are the different symbols?

What conclusion can you draw from this? Do not experiment with the different types of symbols as these will not be shown as you wanted them to be on Internet Explorer.

Complex lists

In Figure 4.2 you saw that you can also use HTML elements as list elements which give rise to new paragraphs. This can also be expressed more generally: You can use almost any HTML element you want as a list element, and consequently other lists as well. You can also subdivide your enumeration points. Nothing in the syntax changes; you must simply use another <UL>-</UL> construct as a list element.

```
<UL>
  <LI>
    Apple
    <UL>
      <LI>Granny Smith</LI>
      <LI>Pomegranate</LI>
    </UL>
  </LI>
  <LI>
    Pear
    <UL>
      <LI>large pear</LI>
      <LI>small pear</LI>
    </UL>
  </LI>
  <LI>
    Orange
    <UL>
      <LI>Blood orange</LI>
      <LI>Valencia orange</LI>
    </UL>
  </LI>
</UL>
```

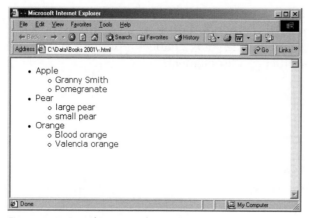

Figure 4.5: Complex unnumbered lists

In Figure 4.5 you can see that the sublists of the unnumbered lists are represented by other symbols. This is also the case in Internet Explorer. You can try to force the symbol type to appear using the TYPE attribute, but this would be like banging your head against a brick wall with Internet Explorer.

In the code you can see that the list elements for apple, pear, and orange all consist of text and an unnumbered list. This list must *not* be separated by <BR> or anything similar, as a list always begins on a new line.

Searching for errors

You should always take care to make it clear which element is on which line by using indents.

```
<UL>
<LI>
Apple
<UL>
<LI>Granny Smith
<UL>
<LI>yellow
<UL>
<LI>1 kg</LI>
<LI>2 kg</LI>
</UL>
```

```
</LI>
<LI>green
<UL>
<LI>1 kg</LI>
<LI>2 kg</LI>
</UL>
</LI>
</LI>
<LI>Pomegranate</LI>
</UL>
</LI>
</UL>
```

Not entirely clear? In the browser (Figure 4.6) you can also see that there must be something wrong somewhere, because the entry pomegranate is in the wrong list.

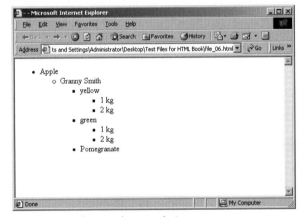

Figure 4.6: Where is the mistake?

If however, you indent the code, you will stumble on the cause of the problems sooner or later: the unnumbered list with the entry yellow and green was not closed with a </UL> tag. The code appears as follows:

```
<UL>
  <LI>
    Apple
    <UL>
```

```
        <LI>Granny Smith
          <UL>
            <LI>yellow
              <UL>
                <LI>1 kg</LI>
                <LI>2 kg</LI>
              </UL>
            </LI>
            <LI>green
              <UL>
                <LI>1 kg</LI>
                <LI>2 kg</LI>
              </UL>
            </LI>
          </UL>
        </LI>
        <LI>pomegranate</LI>
      </UL>
    </LI>
</UL>
```

And the browser shows the list(s) as intended (see Figure 4.7).

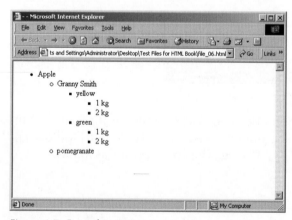

Figure 4.7: Everything is correct now!

> **Note**
>
> *You will have already noticed that the browser runs out of list symbols from the fourth level down. If you want to be more flexible, you have to use graphics for these symbols. In Chapter 6 you will learn more about graphics, and in Chapter 8 you find out how to arrange these graphics so that you can imitate an unnumbered list.*

Numbered lists

This book contains a lot of step-by-step instructions. These instructions are all numbered. As mentioned at the beginning of this chapter, this is not just our own work – much of this process was done automatically by our software package. HTML can also do this!

Creating lists

The creation of a numbered list is carried out in several steps:

1 Create a HTML page.

2 Begin the unnumbered list in the `<BODY>` section with the tag `<OL>` *ordered list*.

3 Now create the individual elements of the list and insert them between `<LI>` and `</LI>`. This stands for *list element*.

4 When you are finished, end the unnumbered list with `</OL>`.

To arrange the following authors in ascending order according to their dates of birth, use the following HTML code (Figure 4.8):

```
<OL>
  <LI>
    Goethe
  </LI>
  <LI>
    Schiller
  </LI>
  <LI>
```

```
    Kleist
  </LI>
  <LI>
    Rowling
  </LI>
</OL>
```

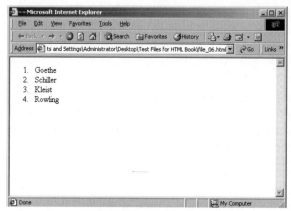

Figure 4.8: A numbered list

What we said at the start of this chapter about unnumbered lists also applies to numbered lists (Figure 4.9):

```
<OL>
  <LI>
    Goethe<BR>
      Wilhelm Meister's Years of Travel
  </LI>
  <LI>
    Schiller<BR>
      William Tell
  </LI>
  <LI>
    Kleist<BR>
      The broken jug
  </LI>
```

```
<LI>

   Rowling<BR>

     mainly Harry Potter

</LI>

</OL>
```

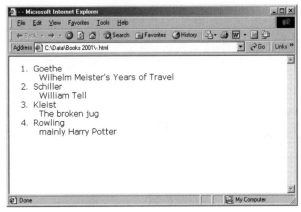

Figure 4.9: The list with breaks (automatic indents)

Types of list

In practice, most lists follow this pattern:

- They have arabic numbers (1, 2, 3,...).

- They begin at number 1.

Sometimes. lists may be different. Here, HTML offers some options which we will now discuss.

First, a list does not have to start with the number 1. Assume that we want (for whatever reason) to begin the list with the value 13. To do so, we have to insert the START attribute and start value (in this case 13) in the <OL> tag:

```
<OL START="13">

   <LI>

      Goethe<BR>

        Wilhelm Meister's Years of Travel

   </LI>

   <LI>

      Schiller<BR>

        William Tell
```

```
  </LI>
  <LI>
    Kleist<BR>
      The Broken Jug
  </LI>
  <LI>
    Rowling<BR>
      mainly Harry Potter
  </LI>
</OL>
```

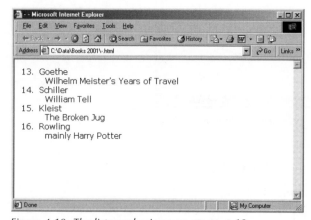

Figure 4.10: The list numbering now starts at 13

You can see the result in Figure 4.10.

Within the list you can also skip numbers. With the VALUE attribute of the <LI> tag you can indicate the value for the element concerned. Counting then continues with the new start value. So, if you give an element the value 24, the next element will have the value 25 (see Figure 4.11).

```
<OL START="13">
  <LI>
    Goethe<BR>
      Wilhelm Meister's Years of Travel
  </LI>
  <LI>
    Schiller<BR>
```

```
          William Tell
  </LI>
  <LI>
    Kleist<BR>
      The Broken Jug
  </LI>
  <LI VALUE="24">
    Rowling<BR>
      mainly Harry Potter
  </LI>
  <LI>
    Wenz/Hauser<BR>
      only subject literature
  </LI>
</OL>
```

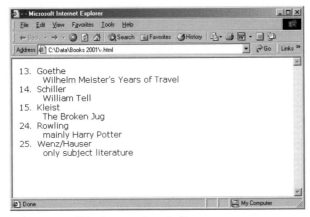

Figure 4.11: Skipping numbers in lists

Numbered lists must always begin at 1. If we now turn to the second restriction, numbering would always be numerical. Again, HTML offers alternatives:

- Numbering in small roman numerals: i, ii, iii, iv, ...

- Numbering in large roman numerals: I, II, III, IV, ...

- Numbering in small letters: a, b, c, ...

- Numbering in large letters: A, B, C, ...

73

In the TYPE attribute of the <OL> tag you can indicate which kind of numbering you would like. If you do not specify your preference, numbers will be used. With i or I, small or large roman numerals will be used, with a or A, small or large letters are used. In the following listing, all the options are shown at the same time (Figure 4.12).

```
<OL>
  <LI>
    Goethe
    <OL TYPE="i">
      <LI>Wilhelm Meister's Years of Teaching</LI>
      <LI>Wilhelm Meister's Years of Travel</LI>
    </OL>
  </LI>
  <LI>
    Schiller
    <OL TYPE="I">
      <LI>William Tell</LI>
      <LI>Macbeth</LI>
    </OL>
  </LI>
  <LI>
    Kleist
    <OL TYPE="a">
      <LI>The Broken Jug</LI>
      <LI>Penthesilea</LI>
    </OL>
  </LI>
  <LI>
    Rowling
    <OL TYPE="A">
      <LI>Harry Potter 1</LI>
      <LI>Harry Potter 2</LI>
      <LI>Harry Potter 3</LI>
      <LI>Harry Potter 4</LI>
```

```
   </OL>

</LI>

<LI>

  Wenz/Hauser

  <OL>

    <LI>EASY Photoshop 6.0</LI>

    <LI>now I am learning

        Dynamic Web-Publishing</LI>

  </OL>

</LI>

</OL>
```

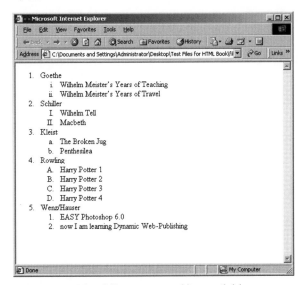

Figure 4.12: The different types of list available

In Figure 4.12, you can see that:

- In numbered lists you can also nest other lists in which you can use other lists as list elements.

- The numbering is not hierarchical, not 1.i, 1.ii, etc.

Mixing lists

You can also use different types of lists nested within a list, for example, a numbered list with an unnumbered list:

```
<OL>
  <LI>
    Goethe
    <UL>
      <LI>Wilhelm Meister's Years of Teaching</LI>
      <LI>Wilhelm Meister's Years of Travel</LI>
    </UL>
  </LI>
  <LI>
    Schiller
    <UL>
      <LI>William Tell</LI>
      <LI>Macbeth</LI>
    </UL>
  </LI>
  <LI>
    Kleist
    <UL>
      <LI>The Broken Jug</LI>
      <LI>Penthesilea</LI>
    </UL>
  </LI>
</OL>
```

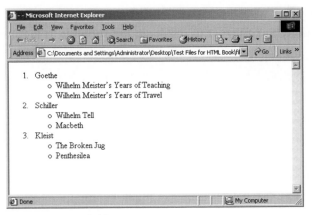

Figure 4.13: Mixed list types

Other lists

HTML offers even more lists. These are not numbered, but provide for a clean layout through automatic indentation, which otherwise you would have to manually carry out using tables (more on this in Chapters 7 and 8).

Definitions lists

A definitions list is used for names and definitions, and for this reason is often used in glossaries. It consists of two elements, the term and its definition. Of course it is up to you what you use definitions lists for, and it doesn't matter to the browser what the content of the individual HTML elements is. You can therefore use the graphic effects for other purposes as well.

In order to create a definitions list, proceed as follows:

1 Create a HTML page.

2 Begin the list (in the <BODY> section of the HTML page) with <DL> – for *definition list*.

3 Insert the term which is to be defined between the <DT> and </DT> tags (*term*).

4 Now insert the definition of the term between the <DD> and </DD> tags (*definition*).

5 Repeat steps 3 and 4 until you have finished listing terms and definitions.

6 End the definitions list with `</DL>`.

Here is an example code: you can see the results in the browser in Figure 4.14:

```
<DL>
   <DT>
     Goethe
   </DT>
   <DD>
     Johann Wolfgang von;
     born in 1749 in Frankfurt/Main
   </DD>
   <DT>
     Schiller
   </DT>
   <DD>
     Friedrich von; born 1759 in Marbach
   </DD>
   <DT>
     Kleist
   </DT>
   <DD>
     Heinrich von; born in 1777 in Frankfurt/Oder
   </DD>
</DL>
```

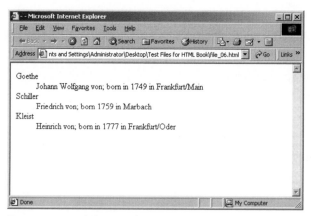

Figure 4.14: A definitions list

If you have installed Netscape Navigator, load the file *bookmark.htm* once again in the browser (this is usually found under C:\Program Files\ Netscape\Netscape 6\defaults\profile\) (Figure 4.15).

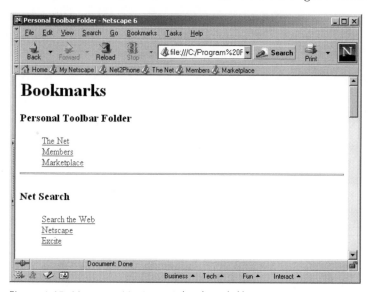

Figure 4.15: Netscape Navigator's bookmark file

Maybe you have already suspected what we are going to say – it looks like a definitions list?! And you are right, here is a (shortened, simplified, and visually improved) extract from the file:

```
<DL>
  <DT><H3>Personal Toolbar Folder</H3>
    <DL>
      <DT>Instant Message</DT>
      <DT>WebMail</DT>
      <DT><H3>Channels</H3>
        <DL>
          <DT>Audio</DT>
          <DT>Cars</DT>
        </DL>
      </DT>
    </DL>
  </DT>
</DL>
```

> **Note**
> *You see – definitions lists can also be nested!*

Formatting lists

The individual elements within a list can be formatted, in the way you already know (Figure 4.16):

```
<DL>
  <DT>
    <B>Goethe</B>
  </DT>
  <DD>
    Johann Wolfgang von;
    <I>born in 1749 in Frankfurt/Main</I>
  </DD>
  <DT>
    <B>Schiller</B>
  </DT>
```

```
<DD>

  Friedrich von; <I>born in 1759 in Marbach</I>

</DD>

<DT>

  <B>Kleist</B>

</DT>

<DD>

  Heinrich von;

  <I>born in 1777 in Frankfurt/Oder</I>

</DD>

</DL>
```

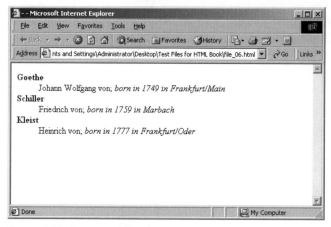

Figure 4.16: Formatted list elements

Numbered lists are, however, a special challenge because if the first word in each list element is written in bold, for example, the numbering symbols are also in bold. The trick here is as follows: Insert the whole list between the appropriate formatting tags. From this it naturally follows that the numbering symbols are formatted in the same way:

```
<B>

<OL>

  <LI>

    Goethe

  </LI>

  <LI>
```

```
    Schiller
  </LI>
  <LI>
    Kleist
  </LI>
  <LI>
    Rowling
  </LI>
</OL>
</B>
```

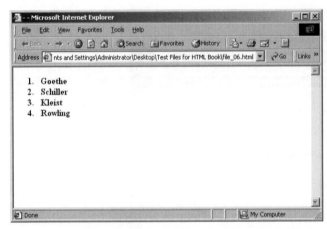

Figure 4.17: The list numbers are in bold, along with the list

As you can see, in Figure 4.17, everything is in bold, which is not always wanted. Unfortunately there is no way out of this dilemma. You can create your list by hand if need be.

If, for example, you want all the list symbols to appear in bold and the list points to appear in bold and italic, this is possible, as shown in Figure 4.18:

```
<B>
<OL>
  <LI>
    <I>Goethe</I>
  </LI>
  <LI>
    <I>Schiller</I>
```

```
    </LI>
    <LI>
      <I>Kleist</I>
    </LI>
    <LI>
      <I>Rowling</I>
    </LI>
  </OL>
</B>
```

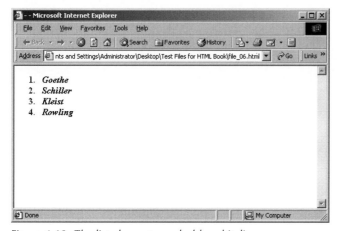

Figure 4.18: The list elements are bold and italic

This chapter has covered lists in detail. Chapter 5 goes on to discuss links.

Chapter 5

Links

A Web page consists of an HTML file and possibly a couple of graphics (more about this in Chapter 6). A Web site, on the other hand, consists of several HTML files which are linked to each other. In this chapter you will learn about links and hyperlinks, how you can set up links, and what options are available to you.

Introduction

For links, the `<A>` tag is used. The A stands for *anchor*.

Syntax

A link has the following construction

```
<A HREF="...">Linktext</A>
```

For the individual elements:

- The link is inserted between the `<A>` tags.

- The `HREF` attribute indicates the link's destination. Examples of this are found throughout this chapter!

- `Linktext` indicates the text that will act as the link.

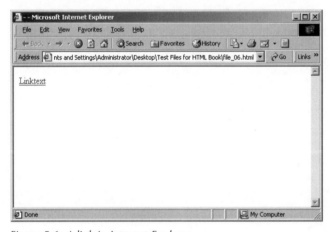

Figure 5.1: A link in Internet Explorer

In Figure 5.1 you see the result: the link text is blue and underlined. If you hover the mouse pointer over it, it changes to a hand. If you click on this link you will be taken to the page it links to. More about this later!

Formatting

If you want to format the link text, the formatting options which you have met before are available. Therefore, you can change the font size and typeface, make the text bold or italic, etc. as follows (Figure 5.2):

```
<P>
Normal Link: <A HREF="">Linktext</A><BR>
Italic Link: <A HREF=""><I>Linktext</I></A><BR>
Bold Link: <A HREF=""><B>Linktext</B></A><BR>
Larger Link:
<A HREF=""><FONT SIZE="+1">Linktext</FONT></A><BR>
Smaller Link:
<A HREF=""><FONT SIZE="-1">Linktext</FONT></A>
</P>
```

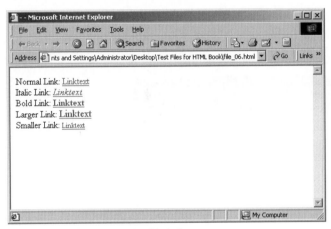

Figure 5.2: Different kinds of link formatting

In order to change the colour of the link, use the COLOR attribute of the <FONT> tag.

```
<A HREF=""><FONT COLOR="Red">Linktext</FONT></A>
```

If you want to set the colour of the link the same for the whole document, use the fixed parameters for the <BODY> tag. The following are available:

- LINK – colour of a link that has not been clicked on
- ALINK – colour of a link whilst it is clicked on by the mouse
- VLINK – colour of a link that has already been clicked

Look at the following example code, displayed in Figure 5.3:

```
<HTML>
<HEAD>
<TITLE>Linkcolours</TITLE>
</HEAD>
<BODY LINK="Red"
      ALINK="White"
      VLINK="Blue"
      BGCOLOR="White">
<A HREF="">click me</A>
</BODY>
</HTML>
```

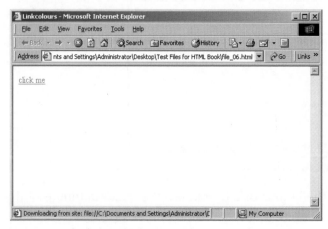

Figure 5.3: The link in the browser (shown in red)

If you click on the link it becomes white (and thus invisible).

Internal links

If you want to link to other Web sites, there are two options: either this Web site is one of your own pages (and therefore from the same server), or it is someone else's page (for example a link to the homepage of a publishing house). As an example, we have given the structure of a fictitious Web site in Figure 5.4.

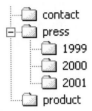

Figure 5.4: The directory tree of the (fictitious) Web site

We assume furthermore, that there is a file *index.html* in each of the given lists, as well as a file *info.html*. From these assumptions, we will now show the different available links.

Links in the same directory

Assume that you are on the page *index.html* in the *product* directory (see Figure 5.4), and want to link to *info.html*. Do it like this:

```
<A HREF="info.html"> goes to info.html</A>
```

So, you simply type the file name, and the link is activated! You can also refer back to the file *index.html* from the file *info.html*, of course:

```
<A HREF="index.html">back to index.html</A>
```

So far, so good. Something that is more difficult, but still quite simple, is linking to files in other directories. Here, there are a number of options.

Relative links

Directory names are divided up by hyphens. In Windows the hyphen is the back slash (\), in Unix/Linux the forward slash (/), in Macintosh the colon (:). In a Web server it is always a forward slash. If you want to refer to a file which is in a different directory to the current file, you have to indicate the route to the new file through the directory path, and separate the names of the individual directories from each other using a forward slash.

We will begin with a simple example: We are on the page *index.html* in the main directory of the Web server, and want to call up the file *index.html* in the *press* directory. The link may then look like the following:

```
<A HREF="press/index.html">To the press region</A>
```

If the Web server is configured in a way such that the file *index.html* is loaded automatically from typing the directory name, the following code is used:

```
<A HREF="press/">To the press region</A>
```

As a rule, it is better to link directly to the file name.

Now, here is a more complicated example. The file *info.html* in the subdirectory `2001` of the `press` directory is to be linked to the file *index.html* in the main directory. The following HTML code processes this:

```
<A HREF="press/2001/info.html">2001</A>
```

So you can see that directory names and file names which are linked to each other are separated from each other by forward slashes.

To date, you have only seen how to get one or several directories deeper into the directory tree. The route back has not yet been shown. There are two particular "directory names" with which this is possible:

* . – describes the current directory
* .. – describes the higher directory

The single point of the detail of the current directory is rarely used. Assume that you are in the file *info.html* in the main directory of the Web server and want to link to the file *index.html* in the same directory. You can then do the following:

```
<A HREF="./index.html">To the start page</A>
```

The following shortened form is also possible as an alternative with the appropriate configuration of the Web server. As no file name is indicated, the Web server automatically supplies *index.html*:

```
<A HREF="./">to the start page</A>
```

Now to something really interesting: the jump back. We are in the file *info.html* in the subdirectory `2001` of the *press* directory and want to link to the file *index.html* in the *press* directory. This directory is the one directly above, so:

```
<A HREF="../index.html">to the press region</A>
```

This shortened form is normally possible with the appropriate Web server configuration:

```
<A HREF="../">to the press region</A>
```

In order to now jump back several directories, you must use double points several times. So, in order to link the file *info.html* in the directory *press/2001* to the file *index.html* in the main directory, use the following code:

```
<A HREF="../../index.html">To the main page</A>
```

Alternatively, you can, of course, also use the following shortened form with most Web servers:

```
<A HREF="../../">To the main page</A>
```

If you now want to jump to the contact region (*index.html*) from the press region (as before: file *press/2001/info.html*) you can use the same technique:

```
<A HREF="../../contact/index.html">to the contact region</A>
```

Or the shortened form:

```
<A HREF="../../contact/">To the contact area</A>
```

What happens here?

1. To begin with, we are in the directory *press/2001*.

2. Through the first `../` we jump back one directory to the directory *press*.

3. Through the second `../` we jump back one more directory, into the main directory.

4. Through *contact/* we change to the *contact* directory.

5. Through *index.html* the file *index.html* is called up.

Absolute links

The referencing technique described above is known as *relative* referencing since all references are indicated as relative to the present point of view, and therefore begin with a file name or a directory name.

With *absolute* links, on the other hand, the reference begins with a forward slash (/). This is a reference to the main directory of the Web server. You have to therefore indicate the whole name of the file that you want to link to.

If this sounds too theoretical for you, here are a few examples:

From any place, link to the file *index.html* in the main directory in your application as follows:

```
<A HREF="/index.html">To the main page</A>
```

In an appropriately configured Web server, the following also applies, without giving details of the file name:

```
<A HREF="/">To the main page</A>
```

From every page in your application, link to the file *info.html* in the directory *press/2001* as follows:

```
<A HREF="/press/2001/info.html">Press 2001</A>
```

If you are in the directory *products* in the file *index.html*, you can refer to the file *info.html* in the same directory in the following ways:

1. Directly through the filename:

```
<A HREF="info.html">Linktext</A>
```

2. Relative:

```
<A HREF="./info.html">Linktext</A>
```

3. Absolute:

```
<A HREF="/products/info.html">Linktext</A>
```

Which links should you use?

However, which kind of links should you use — relative or absolute ("direct" links with files in the same directory are strictly speaking also relative links)?

Absolute links have the advantage that they are identical in every single page, and every single directory. They can link from everywhere by using a forward slash on the main page. If you use the same header in all your pages (for example, your firm's logo) and link all of your homepages, absolute links are a bad idea. You can see at `http://www.google.com`: the header graphic is the same everywhere and uses absolute links (see emphasis in Figure 5.5).

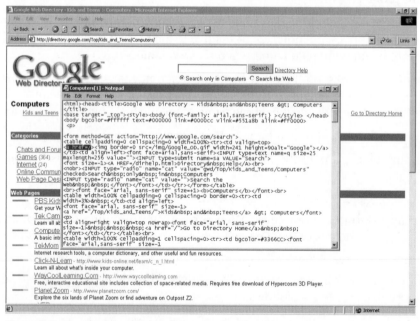

Figure 5.5: Google uses absolute links

With relative links it is the opposite: because the links are relative to the memory of the current file, moving a single directory is usually problematic: the relative links on higher directories no longer work. On the other hand, relative links also have their advantages: the link "*info.html*" clearly takes less effort to type than the link "*/press/2001/info.html*".

We look at two possible scenarios. First, the press region in our publishing company example. The marketing department has established that in addition to press releases, current news should also be offered. As a result there is a new directory */news* and this directory becomes the subdivided directory *press*. Things may then look roughly like Figure 5.6.

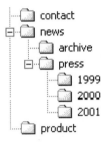

Figure 5.6: The new directory structure

What will you now discover when you try out existing links?

- No absolute links *in* the *press* directory work any more.

- All other absolute links continue to work.

- All relative links (completely) inside the *press* directory or (completely) outside the *press* directory continue to work.

- Relative links from the *press* directory to outside or vice versa do not work.

Continuing in the same example, what happens if the publishing company merges with another company? Under a new name (if possible with *.com* in the company's title), the new company tries to dominate the market. Its new Web site is actually a portal page with two directories. The first contains the publisher's existing Web pages, the second contains the new partner's Web pages (see Figure 5.7).

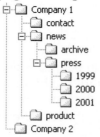

Figure 5.7: The new directory structure

A look at the links brings the following to light:

- No absolute links work now.

- All relative links (completely) inside the individual applications (directory *Company1* or *Company2*) continue to work.

You can conclude from this that relative lists are usually the best option, even if the second scenario is more improbable than the first. It often helps to have a third option: always use relative links, apart from if you link to your homepage, when you always use */* or */index.html*.

External links

At the beginning of the World Wide Web there were link lists. Everyone put references to their favourite pages online, because at this point, graphics were little used due to the lack of an infrastructure and the slow speed of systems. Today, of course, this is different, Web sites must sparkle and crash, colours rule, and link lists are more easily pushed into the background. Nevertheless, the good old *external link* is not dead.

HTTP links

If you want to link to another Web site on another server, you have to give the entire name – the server name, directory, and the file name. To link to the homepage of the publisher of this book, use:

```
<A HREF="http://www.pearsoned.com/">Pearson Education</A>
```

What is actually used is the shortened form, because as you see, we have withheld the file name. The following form would have been more detailed:

```
<A HREF="http://www.pearsoned.com/index.html"
>Pearson Education</A>
```

You can link to subdirectories in the same way. The following link, for example, refers the visitor to the contact us page of the publisher:

```
<A HREF="http://www.pearsoned.com/contactUs.htm"
>Pearson Education Contact</A>
```

FTP links

FTP stands for *File Transfer Protocol* and is the Internet protocol for file transfers over the World Wide Web. Of course, you can transfer files using the conventional HTTP protocol (HyperText Transfer Protocol), so FTP is more suitable for this purpose. For example, uncompleted downloads can often be resumed again at the place where they were broken off, instead of having to start them over again. If, then, you want to download software from the Internet and have the choice between a HTTP and a FTP link, you should usually choose the FTP server.

Nothing is changed in the syntax of the link, apart from the fact that you have to use `ftp` as a protocol marker:

```
<A HREF="ftp://ftp.microsoft.com/">FTP server
  Microsoft</A>
```

Of course, you can also link directly to files on the FTP server (this site is only used as an example - it does not exist!):

```
<A HREF="ftp://ftp.microsoft.com/whistler.exe">
  The new Windows version free to download!</A>
```

In the FTP protocol, commands for authorisation are installed via username and password. Most FTP servers allow so-called *anonymous* *access* to their data. This means that `anonymous` is sent as the username, and the email address of the user is used as a password.

If a connection demands a password, you can indicate this password clearly in the link:

```
<A
 HREF="ftp://user:password@ftp.server.uk/">
FTP</A>
```

Newsgroups

In the old days, when the World Wide Web only played a small part in the Internet, most of what appeared on the Internet was email or newsgroups. A newsgroup is a worldwide discussion forum. Using email, you can post a question to a newsgroup and someone on the other side of the world might answer you. Newsgroups are divided up hierarchically into several groups (Figure 5.8).

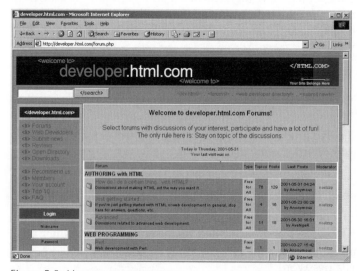

Figure 5.8: Newsgroup messages

We won't go any further into this matter here, as this is an HTML book, after all. However, we want to show you how you can address a link to a newsgroup. As an example, we have found a newsgroup on HTML. The newsgroup is called *Authoring with HTML*, and contains a large number of *postings* (messages posted by newsgroup users). If you want to link directly to this newsgroup, use the following link:

```
<A HREF="Authoring with HTML">
to HTML-Newsgroup</A>
```

Caution

Make sure that no / / follows news!

Newsgroups are stored on many servers worldwide. If a message is published on one server, this is passed on to other servers. On the other hand, all servers accommodate all newsgroups. You need a special program to read news, a *newsreader*. This program is integrated in most browsers (or can be downloaded).

Mail links

Internet magazines report this again and again: many companies make it very difficult for visitors to their Web sites to get in contact with them. And it's so simple to do!

An email link works in the following way: as soon as the user clicks on it, his default mail program is activated and the user can begin to type. Here is the simplest form of link:

```
<A HREF="mailto:paul@cybertechnics.co.uk">Mail to
   P. Watkinson</A>
```

By clicking on this link, a mail window is opened and paul@cybertechnics.co.uk is set as the recipient (see Figure 5.9). You can thus email the editor of this book like this.

Figure 5.9: A mail window with a predefined recipient

You can also address your email to several recipients if you separate them from each other with commas:

```
<A HREF="mailto:paul@cybertechnics.co.uk,info@cybertechnics
.co.uk">
```
```
Mail to several</A>
```

Now a few words about "unofficial tricks". Mail links offer some possibilities which are not intended in the official specification, but nevertheless work in most browsers. You can attach a lot more options to the recipient's email address according to the following code:

```
<A HREF="mailto:paul@cybertechnics.co.uk?option1=abc&
➡option2=def&option3=ghi">
Mail </A>
```

The following options are available:

- bcc= – (blind carbon copy) copies a recipient into the email (their email address will be hidden)

- cc= – (carbon copy) copies another recipient into the email

- subject= – the subject matter of the email

- body= – the text of the email

Here is a detailed link which uses all of these options:

```
<A HREF="mailto:paul@cybertechnics.co.uk?
cc=info@cybertechnics.co.uk&bcc=jonathan@yahoo.com&subject=
➥EASY HTML&body=a great book!">Mail to Cybertechnics</A>
```

As you can gather from Figure 5.10 – it works! Although it doesn't work with every browser, and a mail program must of course be available for the user. The most important detail is the email address of the recipient.

Figure 5.10: Addressing and writing an email

Downloads

If you want to download software or other files, you can use the normal syntax. You do not refer to an HTML page, but to the appropriate file. Depending on the configuration of your browser, the file is then opened directly by the browser (for example PDF files (Portable Document Format, a format that can be read by Adobe Acrobat Reader which is pre-installed on all new PCs)) or in the application which belongs to it (for example, word-processing documents), or the browser asks you where the file should be saved on your hard disk (Figure 5.11). You can use any method already introduced for the link itself.

```
<A HREF="downloads/file.zip">file.zip</A>
```

Figure 5.11: Choosing whether to save a file to your hard disk or run the program

Text markers

It is not only HTML pages that can be linked to, but also specific areas of a page. You often see the following on a Web page: right at the bottom there is a link "to the top" which scrolls straight to the top of the page. This happens with the aid of a little HTML.

You can put a text marker on to an HTML page in the same way as a position marker. This marker is not shown in the browser, but it is clear where it is. You insert such a marker as follows:

```
<A NAME="above">Some Text</A>
```

With this, the text mark is defined. In order to define a text marker at the top of a page, you use the heading as text, or you insert an empty character inside the <A> element.

The name of a text mark has to fulfil the following requirements, so that it works in all browsers:

- It must not consist of letters a-z or A-Z.

- In particular it must not contain any blanks (the Internet Explorer does not like this).

- Special characters (for example foreign characters) are forbidden.

Now, to refer to a text marker, simply link to it! To make it clear that this is a text marker and not a file, put a hash sign (#) in front of the name of the text marker:

```
<A HREF="#above">to the top</A>
```

In the following listing you see the whole thing in an example. On this page there is a lot of text, so the heading is no longer visible if you are at the end of the text. Clicking on the link jumps you back to the top of the page (Figures 5.12 and 5.13):

```
<HTML>
<HEAD>
  <TITLE>Text marker</TITLE>
</HEAD>
<BODY BGCOLOR="white">
<A NAME="top">
<H2>Wilhelm Meister's Years of Travel</H2>
</A>
<P>
   Man is a limited being. Sundays are devoted <BR>
to reconsidering our restrictions. It is material <BR>
sufferings that we barely notice during the frenzy <BR>
of the week, so we immediately consult the doctor. <BR>
If our restrictions are economic and even civic, so our <BR>
professionals are required to observe their agenda. <BR>
If that which plagues us is intellectual or moral, so <BR>
we have a friend,a confidante to whom to turn,and whose <BR>
advice and influence to seek: enough, that is the law: <BR>
nobody may prolong a worry or grievance into the new week.
<BR>
</P>
<P><A HREF="#top">to the top</A></P>
</BODY>
</HTML>
```

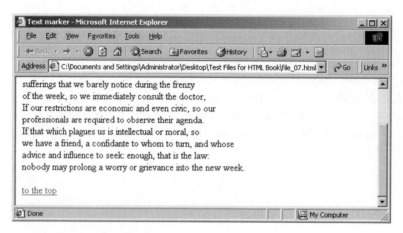

Figure 5.12: The link at the bottom of the page jumps...

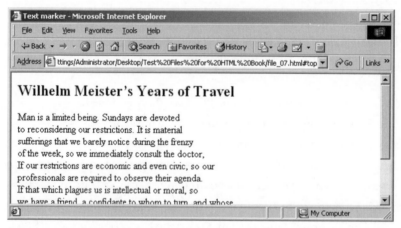

Figure 5.13: ... back to the top of the page!

Longer pages can be subdivided like this. Every point is linked to the appropriate section of the page so they can be directly jumped to. An example of this is Netscape 6's *Release Notes* (see Figure 5.14). At the top of the page are the most important points which can be jumped to using text markers.

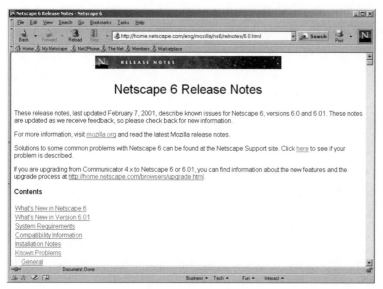

Figure 5.14: Netscape 6's release notes

Here is an extract from the code:

```
<ul>
<li>
<font face="Arial,Helvetica">
<font color="#000000"><a href="#whatnew">What's
New in This Release</a></font></font></li>

<li>
<font face="Arial,Helvetica">
<font color="#000000"><a href="#install">Before
You Install</a></font></font></li>

<li>
<font face="Arial,Helvetica">
<font color="#000000"><a href="#geniss">General
Issues</a></font></font></li>

...
```

Look at the first link, `What's New In This Release`. This refers to a text marker called *whatnew* and we find this in the code below:

```
<p><a NAME="whatnew"></a>
<h2>
<font face="Arial,Helvetica">
<font color="#000000"><font size=+1>What's
New in This Release</font></font></font></h2>
. . .
```

You also see that professional pages are put together simply. At the same time, note that the text marker has no content, which is not best practice, but is tolerated by most browsers.

You can also directly link to text markers from other pages. To do this, you use the techniques that we have introduced in this chapter, and attach the text marker to the file name. The following link leads, for example, directly to the Netscape text marker we have just looked at:

```
<A HREF="http://home.netscape.com/eng/mozilla/ns6/relnotes/
➡6.0.html#whatnew">What's new in Netscape 6-?</A>
```

Target window — to open another window

This section will briefly discuss another point which is introduced in Chapter 10. Normally, when links in the current window are opened, you can then activate links in the new window. To do so, you use the `TARGET` attribute of the `<A>` tag. You now have two options:

- `_self` – loads the target of the link in the current window (default setting). w tym serwm
- `_blank` – loads the target of the link in a new browser window.
- `any`– loads the target of the link in a new browser window, unless, the name *any* has already been used, then the target is loaded in this window. kwe open

There are two options:

```
<A HREF="http://www.pearsoned.co.uk" TARGET="_blank">
  Pearson Education</A><BR>
```

```
<A HREF="http://www.idg.co.uk" TARGET="_blank">
  IDG</A><BR>
<A HREF="http://www.awl.co.uk" TARGET="_blank">
  Addison-Wesley</A>
```

every time *move demo*

No matter how often you click on any link, the browser will load a new window every time. It is different in the following example:

```
<A HREF="http://www.pearsoned.uk" TARGET="new">
  Pearson Education</A><BR>
<A HREF="http://www.idg.com" TARGET="new">
  IDG</A><BR>
<A HREF="http://www.awl.co.uk/" TARGET="new">
  Addison-Wesley</A>
```

first time and then in the same window ↳ end

The first click on a link loads a new window; all further clicks load the same new window because the window name *new* is associated with the loaded window.

You can automatically load all links in a particular window if you type <BASE TARGET="new"> in the <HEAD> section of the HTML page. This applies to all links, unless you explicitly indicate the TARGET attribute in a link.

```
<HTML>
<HEAD>
  <TITLE>TARGET</TITLE>
  <BASE TARGET="new">
</HEAD>
<BODY BGCOLOR="white">
<H3>A choice of links</H3>
<A HREF="http://www.pearsoned.co.uk" TARGET="_self">
  Pearson Education</A><BR>
<A HREF="http://www.idg.com">IDG</A><BR>
<A HREF="http://www.awl.co.uk">Addison-Wesley</A>
</BODY>
</HTML>
```

By using <BASE TARGET="new"> the targets of all links are loaded in a new window called *new*. An exception of this is the link to *Pearson Education*, because it will be loaded in the current window. `target="_self"` overwrites the handicap with `<BASE TARGET>` (Figure 5.15).

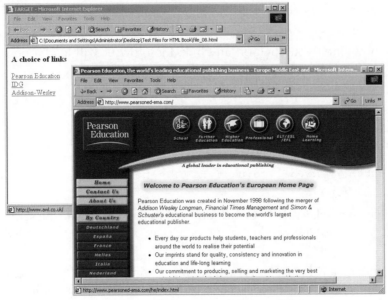

Figure 5.15: (Almost) all links are loaded in the new window

Legalities

Normally Web sites are happy to be linked to from other sites, because this is a virtual free advertisement for him. Nevertheless, there are some cases where people would be unhappy to see a link:

- In connection with negative remarks ("I bought the broken equipment from XY" together with a link to the homepage of company XY)

- Links in the middle of a server (so-called *deep links*, not on the main site) (this process is under consideration in the United States).

- Links to sites with dubious content, such as pornagraphic sites.

The legal position concerning the last point is not yet clear in the UK. Lots of Web sites manage to include the explanation: "external link: we are not responsible for the content of an external Web site" with links from their site.

Such a sentence may be a good idea for your Web site as well. And, if possible, ask permission if you link to a foreign Web server!

Chapter 6

Graphics

At least 99% of all Web sites use graphics, whether they are attractive or not. A picture, used correctly, so the saying goes, is worth more than a thousand words. This chapter clarifies which file formats can be used in HTML (in the Web), and for which purposes. Then we will show you how to install graphics in HTML code using the <IMG> tag. To conclude, we will discuss image maps, subdividing an example photograph into different areas and providing these with links.

File formats

On the Web, there are three file formats commonly used for bitmap graphics: GIF, JPEG and PNG

> **Note**
>
> *'Bitmap graphic' describes a graphic which consists of small dots (pixels). In contrast to this, there are also vector graphics which consist of mathmatically calculated lines and curves held in their place by anchor points.*

Depending on their proposed use, different file formats should be chosen. Table 6.1 gives you more information about the available options. You can find more detailed information about the individual formats later in this chapter.

Abbreviation	Stands for	Transparency	Colour depth	Compression	Areas of use
GIF	Compuserve Graphics Interchange Format	Yes	Max. 8 bit; this represents 256 colours	Loss-free-compression, which primarily compresses colour areas as well	Graphics with bigger areas of colour, buttons, text, etc.
JPEG	Joint Picture Experts Group	No	24 bit; this represents 16 million colours	Dissipating compression	Photos, graphics with lots of colour
PNG	Portable Network Graphic	Yes	To 8 bit (PNG-8); 24 bit (PNG-24)	Loss-free	Can be used in all areas

Table 6.1: Graphics file formats for the Web

GIF

The GIF-format (*CompuServe Graphics Interchange*) was originally developed by CompuServe. It uses the same compression that is used in zip files, for example. This algorithm is compressed *loss-free*. This means that no image information (or quality) is lost when it is compressed.

GIF is the most common graphics format on the Web. It only offers a maximum of 256 colours (8 bit), however, but most of the elements of a Web site are represented well. The question is, according to what criteria does one choose the number and the variety of colours needed in an image? The rule is, generally, the fewer colours there are, the smaller the graphic file will be.

If an image originally consists of more colours than necessary, the image will be *dithered* by the reduction of the colour depth. What is *dithering*? Dithering means that individual colour values are replaced by other similar colour values. Adjacent colour pixels are changed so that the colour values that are left out are simulated, thus the final quality of the graphic will not be as good.

The next question is, which of the 256 possible colours will be included? This depends strongly on the appearance of the graphic. If the graphic consists of less than 256 colours, for example, it makes most sense to take on the exact colour values of the graphic. If you want an authentic representation of the figure on different platforms (Windows and Mac) on a computer with a resolution of just 8 bits (256 colours), it is best to use the Web-safe palette. This consists of 216 colours which are available on Macs and Windows with a very low colour depth. This means that graphics will appear as your intended them to for the maximum number of users.

> **Tip**
>
> *The Web-safe palette only works with images which have relatively few colours. Because most computers have a high colour depth, it is hardly ever used. Its importance could increase, however, with the use of mobile terminals with lower resolution and with colour display.*

Until now, you have only heard that the GIF format is restricted to relatively few colours, and is compressed without loss of quality. All this does not explain its popularity. A special function that GIF offers is that a colour can be changed to transparent. This colour is then not shown in the browser. By doing this, you are able, for example, to create graphics which can be placed on any different background colour.

Another function which has contributed to the popularity of the GIF format is the option of saving animations. These GIF animations are actually a succession of GIF images which are saved in one file. In addition to this, you can adapt every single image of the animation (often called a frame), as long as it is displayed. GIF animations can be comfortably adapted with Adobe ImageReady (with Photoshop), Ulead GIF Animator, and many other programs.

JPEG

The JPEG-format (*Joint Picture Experts Group*) is used mainly for photos. It has lossy compression, which breaks down complex photos into smaller file sizes. In doing so, quality is lost (hence 'lossy').

When you save an image as a JPEG, the graphics program offers you several quality levels. 1 is the lowest level; here, the images are very poor quality. In the highest level the file sizes are very large, but file quality is correspondingly better.

> **Note**
>
> *In the highest quality level, compression also results in quality loss. For this reason, you should save an image in another format during the editing process, and only save it as a JPEG right at the end.*

PNG

The PNG format (*Portable Network Graphic*; pronounced Ping) is so new that it has not yet gained widespread acceptance. It was created to overcome the licensing problems which exist with the GIF format. The original goal of the PNG Consortium was to define a graphics format with the same capacity and quality as GIF. The result of this is that some extra functions have been added.

PNG also supports a colour depth of 24 bits (16 million colours), and this is called PNG-24. As well as this, PNG also offers several transparent colours and, like GIF, is also suitable for animations. In contrast, GIF offers a higher performance in the first stage of image construction.

How does the support and circulation of PNG now look? Unfortunately, quite miserable. It is supported by the big browsers Internet Explorer and Netscape Navigator. This has not yet led to a wide distribution, however. The reasons for this may be as follows:

- The functional difference between PNG and GIF formats is not particularly big. Therefore, the incentive to change is not particularly high.

- PNG is not supported by older browsers. If you want your Web site to be seen properly by the maximum number of users, you have to make do without PNG.

- Finally, the PNG formate is not yet well known.

The <IMG> tag

In this section we tie in graphics with HTML. The <IMG> tag is used for this (IMG stands for image). It is one of the few tags that doesn't have to be completed.

The <IMG> tag contains some attributes that have different options. The SRC attribute fixes the image source, HEIGHT and WIDTH control the size, and BORDER determines the display frame. Each one of these attributes has a section dedicated to it.

The SRC attribute

Without SRC there would be no image. This is because SRC defines the source of the image file. This is the position at which the image is found. SRC functions in the same way as the HREF attribute of a normal link.

```
<IMG SRC="image.jpg">
```

In the above code example, call the file *image.jpg*. It is found in the same directory as the HTML file. If you want to call a file which is in another directory, you have to refer to it.

```
<IMG SRC="graphics/image.jpg">
```

The code line above, for example, refers to an image in the Graphics directory.

Absolute references to URLs are possible with the SRC attribute.

```
<IMG SRC="http://www.idg.com/graphics/image.jpg">
```

In this example, the Web site was linked to in the *Graphics* folder (note that this file does not really exist here).

The BORDER attribute

With SRC we have also already defined an image source. Now we will do some fine tuning. The BORDER attribute establishes the width of the image frame in pixels. How this frame will look depends on the browser you are using.

```
<IMG SRC="image.jpg" BORDER="2">
```

This code example puts a frame two pixels wide around the image (see Figure 6.1).

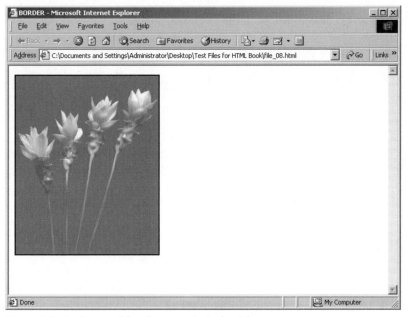

Figure 6.1: A picture with a frame two pixels wide

If you leave out BORDER, no border will appear around the image. One exception is if the image is provided with a link. In this case, it will be displayed with a frame one pixel wide in the normal link colour. In order to get rid of this, you have to set the BORDER to 0.

The HEIGHT and WIDTH attributes

With the HEIGHT and WIDTH attributes you control the size of the image. If the two attributes are not stated, the original size of the image is used. Width and height are normally given in pixels.

Tip

The normal screen resolution is between 800x600 and 1280x1024 pixels. Therefore, you should test your pages to ensure they look good at this resolution.

```
<IMG SRC="image.jpg" HEIGHT="231" WIDTH="350">
```

Our example image is assigned a height of 231 pixels and a width of 350 pixels. As well as indicating the size in pixels, you can also indicate the measurements of an image as a percentage of the size of the browser window.

```
<IMG SRC="image.jpg" HEIGHT="50%" WIDTH="50%">
```

Caution

If you want to change on images proportion, the browser scales the original image. The results of this are not normally good. Therefore, you should distort or scale an image using a graphics program and then import the new image into your Web site.

Figure 6.2 shows the picture shown in Figure 6.1 scaled to 50% of its original height, while keeping 100% of its original width. As you can see, the picture now looks distorted.

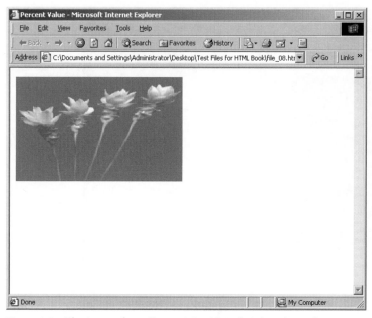

Figure 6.2: The image from Figure 6.1 with its height adjusted

The **NAME** and **ALT** attributes

The NAME attribute establishes a name for the image. This name is used, for example, to call up an image from a script.

```
<IMG SRC="image.jpg" NAME="">
```

You can assign the name Flowers to the image, using the above code. If you now want to call it up in JavaScript, for example, it is enough to indicate the name Flowers.

The ALT attribute sets alternative text to be displayed if the graphic cannot be displayed. This text is also shown if a bigger graphic still has to be loaded, so that the user doesn't get bored and click away from the site. Apart from this, many browsers offer help text in a small yellow box if you hover the mouse over a graphic. The text in this box is also set using the ALT attribute.

```
<IMG SRC="image.jpg" ALT="Flowers">
```

In the above text, the text 'Flowers' would appear in the image placeholder box as the image was downloading (Figure 6.3).

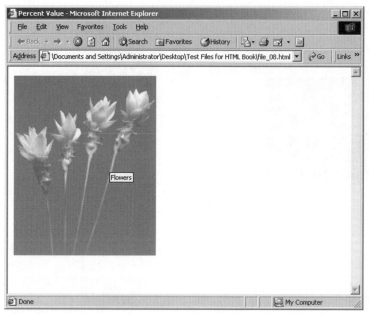

Figure 6.3: The flowers picture with help text in the small box

A new function in HTML 4.0 should be mentioned at this point: the LONGDESC attribute. This indicates that there is a longer description for an image. This is not yet supported by browsers, though.

A short example will explain this:

```
<A NAME="Flowers">Here is a description of the image</A>
<IMG SRC="image.jpg" LONGDESC="#Flowers">
```

A longer descriptive text is written in an anchor to any position. The anchor is provided with a name. For simplicity, in our example, we have put an anchor on the same page as the image in our example. In practice, this function will only be effective if the description is on another page.

The LONGDESC attribute in the <IMG> tag calls up the anchor with the description text. Like a normal link, the referencing is connected to an anchor with a hash sign. Relative and absolute links are also possible to other directories or Web sites.

The ALIGN attribute

The ALIGN attribute lines up text with graphics. In practice, this functionality is used a lot in other texts.

```
<IMG SRC="image.jpg" ALIGN="TOP">any text
```

Some descriptive text is lined up with the top edge of the image, using the above code (Figure 6.4).

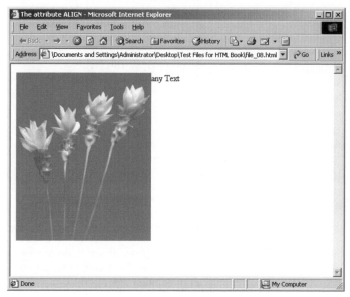

Figure 6.4: Some descriptive text is lined up with the top edge of the image

Note

If you close the <IMG> tag with </IMG>, it makes no difference to the browser whether the text stands inside or outside the <IMG> tags.

Caution

Make sure that the descriptive text next the graphic is not too long. The browser will only accept a maximum of one line of text, and depends on the size of the window on the user's computer. If the text is longer than one line, the rest of the text is shown underneath the graphic. As a rule, you should not give any more than three words or 20 characters for the image label, as the effect is messy otherwise.

119

What different values are there for `ALIGN`? In Table 6.2 you find a list of possible values.

Value for `ALIGN`	Description
`TOP`	Aligns the text with the top edge of the image
`MIDDLE`	Aligns the text with the middle of the image
`BOTTOM`	Aligns the text with the bottom edge of the image
`TEXTTOP` (only Netscape Version 3.0 and higher)	Aligns all the largest text with the top edge of the image. You can see this effect in Figure 6.5
`ABSMIDDLE` (only Netscape Version 3.0 and higher)	Aligns text with the middle of the image. The smallest text is used as the orientation point
`ABSBOTTOM` (only Netscape Version 3.0 and higher)	Aligns the text with the bottom edge of the image. The smallest text acts as an orientation aid
`BASELINE` (only Netscape Version 3.0 and higher)	Corresponds to the `BOTTOM` value

Table 6.2: The possible values of the `ALIGN` attribute

Note

You have probably noticed in our table that the only difference between the "normal" commands like `TOP` *and the "complicated" commands like* `TEXTTOP` *or* `ABSBOTTOM` *is that the complicated commands generally orientate themselves to the smallest text. If you only want to use one text size, there is no problem!*

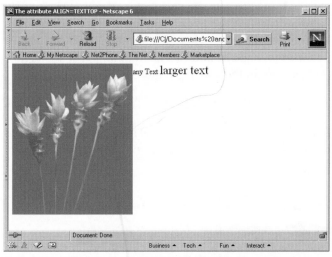

Figure 6.5: Different text sizes aligned with TEXTTOP

The VSPACE and HSPACE attributes

With the VSPACE and HSPACE attributes you can establish the distance of the text from the graphic. The distance is measured in pixels by default. VSPACE (vertical space) determines the distance above and below the graphic, while HSPACE (horizontal space) measures the distances to the left and right of the graphic.

> **Caution**
>
> VSPACE and HSPACE do not differentiate between above and below, and left and right. This means that if you use VSPACE, the text underneath the graphic automatically includes space above and below it. If you want different distances above and below the figure or left and right of the figure, you have to use cascading sheets. These are dealt with in Chapter 10.

The following example shows you how text distances function.

```
<P ALIGN="CENTER">Text above the image</P>

<P ALIGN="CENTER">Text on the left of the image<IMG
➥SRC="image.jpg" ALIGN="ABSMIDDLE" HSPACE="50"
➥VSPACE="50">Text on the right of the image</P>

<P ALIGN="CENTER">Text under the image</P>
```

121

The text above and underneath the image is arranged into its own paragraphs. In the paragraph around the image you find the text left and right of the image. The alignment of the text to the left and right is carried out with `ALIGN="ABSMIDDLE"`. The text above and below the image itself is centre-aligned with `ALIGN="CENTER"` in the `<P>` tag (Figure 6.6).

> **Note**
>
> *Instead of aligning everything to the centre in every paragraph one by one, you can also do it all in one go using a `<DIV>`- or `<CENTER>` tag.*

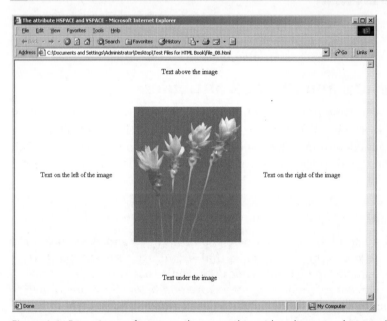

Figure 6.6: Four pieces of text round one graphic with a distance of 50 pixels

Graphics and links

We now refer back to what you learned about links in the last chapter, and learn how to add links to graphics. We use here the Web site of Rhapsody in Bloom (the URL is `http://www.rhapsody-in-bloom.com`). What do you have to do?

The answer is easy: enclose the picture with a link that refers to Rhapsody in Bloom. This is done with the following code:

```
<A HREF="http://www.rhapsody-in-bloom.com">
<IMG SRC="image.jpg">
</A>
```

enclose the picture with a link

You can see the result in Figure 6.7.

Figure 6.7: The flower now has a link, but still has a border

But hold on, we have forgotten to remove the border around the image with BORDER="0". In addition, we can add another alternative descriptive text to it and give it a name.

```
<A HREF="http://www.rhapsody-in-bloom.com">
<IMG SRC="image.jpg" NAME="Flower"
ALT="Rhapsody-in-Bloom" BORDER="0">
</A>
```

Now the picture looks good, and the user knows which site he will jump to because of our help text (Figure 6.8).

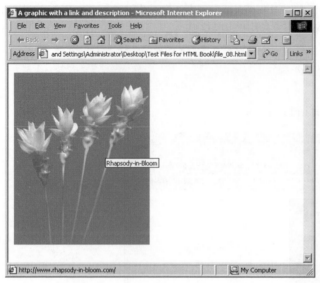

Figure 6.8: The flower links to Rhapsody in Bloom without a border but with a textual description of the link

Note

In the above example we used a direct link. Of course a relative link from another directory to a file in the same directory is also possible. If you want to read again about how this works, see Chapter 5.

Using graphic as a background

The <IMG> tag is not the only place in a HTML page which is suitable for a graphic. The BACKGROUND attribute in the <BODY> tag of the HTML page allows you to set an image as the background for the page. The image is often duplicated across the page if it is too small for the screen. This is known as *tiling* (Figure 6.9).

Figure 6.9: A tiled image

A big advantage of a background image is that you can put any other elements and images on top of it in the foreground. An image can therefore be laid down in different ways. Normally, such effects are only possible with a graphics program.

The code for adding a background image is very easy. We show you how this is done in the complete HTML framework:

```
<HTML>
<HEAD><TITLE>Image as a background</TITLE>
</HEAD>
<BODY BACKGROUND="image.jpg">
Text over the background
</BODY>
</HTML>
```

The source of the image, whether it is relative or absolute, is assigned the BACKGROUND attribute in the <BODY> tag as a value. The normal content of the page stands, as usual, between the <BODY> tags.

Backgrounds

This section is a short excursion in to the options of the BACKGROUND attribute. In the early Web design days it was common to put patterns or (even uglier) lit-up logos in the background. Through the excessive use of this function, the user got sick of seeing this, and Web designers went back to using a white background. This is still the case today. Most "big" Web sites use only one colour for their background, mostly white, to ensure clarity and visual comfort for the user.

Backgrounds have, however, found their niche, mainly in artistic and creative areas. Here, background structures are experimented with, as well as textures and unusual objects. An example of this is: using the bark of a tree as a structure, and then adding a knothole as an image.

If you want to work with backgrounds, you must be careful of several things:

- The background must not be boring and monotone. Bring in interest as foreground images.

- If you make a very big background image that will take up the whole screen (1280x1024 pixels), keep an eye on the size of the file size. More than 30 to 50 KB is not acceptable, and will download very slowly.

- Cut out the background image carefully. You can simulate the tile effect with a graphics program, such as Adobe Photoshop.

Image maps

The last section of this chapter shows you how to divide up an image into several regions and provide them with links. In HTML, a function called *Image map* serves this purpose. The image map is enclosed by <MAP> and </MAP>. A part of the map is a region, enclosed by the <AREA> and </AREA> tags. Anything in this region can be linked to.

> ### Note
>
> *You can choose from client and server page image maps. At this point we are dealing with client page maps which are found inside the HTML page (server page image maps, as the name suggests, run on the server).*

As a practice example for this section we have found a world map (Figure 6.10). On this map we want to select the individual continents and add links to them.

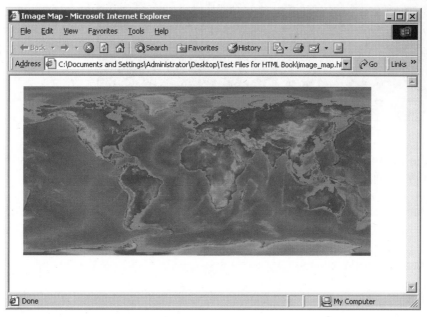

Figure 6.10: A world map

We have not defined the image map by hand, but using a program made for this purpose, Hotmetal Pro. This is easier than putting in every corner point by hand. In Figure 6.11 you see the world map with the Hotmetal image map.

> Tip
>
> *Almost every editor and many graphics programs (Adobe ImageReady, Macromedia Fireworks) allow you to create image maps. Whoever draws image maps manually these days has far too much time on their hands! If you really have no suitable graphics program, use a graphics program with a co-ordination system to measure the image.*

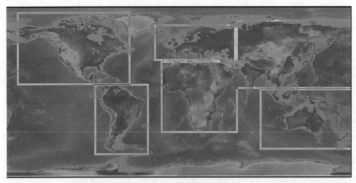

Figure 6.11: The world map with a Hotmetal Pro image map

In the following code we want to show you how an image map works in theory, using the source code produced by Hotmetal.

```
<IMG SRC="world.gif" WIDTH="532" HEIGHT="252"
➥USEMAP="#map">

<MAP NAME="map">

    <AREA SHAPE="RECT" COORDS="394,122,560,212"
➥HREF="oceans.htm">

    <AREA SHAPE="RECT" COORDS="358,19,536,121"
➥HREF="asia.htm">

    <AREA SHAPE="RECT" COORDS="231,26,356,79"
➥HREF="europe.htm" ALT="Europe">

    <AREA SHAPE="RECT" COORDS="241,81,359,187"
➥HREF="africa.htm">

    <AREA SHAPE="RECT" COORDS="18,7,193,115"
➥HREF="northamerica.htm">

    <AREA SHAPE="RECT" COORDS="139,115,221,220"
➥HREF="southamerica.htm">

</MAP>
```

First you see the `<IMG>` tag with the image in the source code. The definition of the image source and size is already known from the previous section. The USEMAP attribute is new. It contains a hash sign and the name of the image map.

The next element in the source text is the <MAP> tag. The start of the image map is signalled by this. The NAME attribute allocate the name to the image map, which also acts as a reference for the <IMG> tag. With NAME, you establish the name of the image map. It is always called up with its name in the <IMG> tag.

Now the individual regions follow, up until the </MAP> tag. We want to take Europe as an example here:

```
<AREA SHAPE="RECT" COORDS="231,26,356,79" HREF="europe.htm"
ALT="Europe">
```

The <AREA> tag represents an area. There are several tags within this tag. SHAPE determines the form of the area: RECT is a rectangle, CIRCLE is a circle and POLYGON is a polygon. The attribute COORDS establishes the co-ordinates of an area. These are separated with commas. Depending on the form, they produce different co-ordination patterns. An x/y co-ordination system is formed with the origin in the top left corner of the image. This corner therefore has the co-ordinates 0/0. Table 6.3 describes the forms and the basic co-ordination system.

SHAPE (Form)	COORDS (co-ordinates)
RECT (Rectangle)	$x_{lio}, y_{lio}, x_{reu}, x_{reu}$ x-and y-co-ordinates of the top left corner; then x- and y-co-ordinates of the bottom right corner
CIRCLE (circle)	x_m, y_m, r x- and y-co-ordinates of the centre and the radius of the circle
POLYGON (polygon)	$x_1, y_1, x_2, y_2, ... x_n, y_n$ x- and y-co-ordinates of the first, the second... and the nth point
DEFAULT	Applies to all areas which do not occur in the <AREA>- tag. Therefore co-ordinates are not required

Table 6.3: Form and co-ordinates of an area in an image map

The next attribute is HREF. It says which pages will be linked to if the user clicks on an area in the image map. The link can be relative or absolute. Here, it refers to a file in the same directory called *europe.htm.*

The last attribute is ALT. It defines a description and help text for the area. If you hover the mouse over the area, the text is shown in a yellow help box.

Caution

The ALT attribute only works in IE Version 4 and NN Version 6 onwards.

Chapter 7

Tables I

You are probably familier with tables from your word-processing or spreadsheet program. In HTML, tables have two different functions. On the one hand, they can be used as visible tables as layout elements for data. On the other hand, invisible tables are also used in the placing of elements, including how to place elements on layers. In this chapter we explain the basic functions of tables.

The structure of tables

A table consists of individual cells. These are divided up into lines and columns by tags. We now show you, step by step, how to construct a table:

1 First define whether it is a table. The `<TABLE>` tag serves this purpose. A table is completed with the `</TABLE>` tag. The individual lines are contained in this tag pair.

2 The tag for a line is `<TR>` ("table row"). Line text is completed within with the `</TR>` tag.

```
<TABLE>

<TR></TR>

</TABLE>
```

column

3 This just leaves the cells. They are completed with the `<TD>` and `</TD>` ("table data") tags.

```
<TABLE>

<TR><TD></TD></TR>

</TABLE>
```

4 Next you add any text you want in the cells between `<TD>` and `</TD>`. The number of cells in a line also determines the number of rows.

> **Caution**
>
> *Content, whether images or text, can only be added within the `<TD>` tags. Text which is not between the `<TD>` tags will either be wrongly displayed or not displayed at all.*

In the next example we have created a simple table with two columns and two rows (Figure 7.1).

```
<TABLE BORDER="1">

<TR>

<TH>Head column 1</TH>

<TH>Head column 2</TH>

</TR>

<TR>
```

```
<TD>cell 1</TD>
<TD>cell 2</TD>
</TR>
</TABLE>
```

> **Note**
>
> *For this example we have allocated a width of one pixel to the attribute* BORDER *so that the table is visible in the browser.*

Figure 7.1: A simple table

In this example you can see something special, namely the <TH> and </TH> tags. They stand for head cells. They work differently to the <TD> tag only in that the text within them is displayed in bold and is centred in the cell.

> **Note**
>
> *The* <TH> *tag is not common any more. The corresponding tags (for bold* <B> *for example; for centre aligning, the* ALIGN="CENTER" *attribute) or stylesheets are normally used for formatting.*

The columns of a table in HTML are determined by the number of cells in a line. In order to correctly program a table, every line must have the same number of cells. Alternatively, several cells can be bound together (see the section on "Binding cells"). Different numbers of cells in individual lines are the biggest cause of formatting mistakes in the creation of tables.

The width and height of tables

In this section we show you how you can establish the width and height of a table. You will then learn how to change the height and width of a cell and fit this into the table.

The width and height of a table depends first on the content of the cell. If you give no instruction as to the width and height, the table will be the exact width of the whole of the text and perhaps available images will fit into it. If, on the other hand, you specify a particular width and height, and the contents no longer fit into the table because, for example, an image is too big, the table is adapted to accommodate the contents.

Now we want to show you how to specify the width and height using the attributes WIDTH and HEIGHT in the <TABLE> tag. You can give these measurements in pixels or as a percentage. Pixels are image points. The number of image points that are shown on your monitor depends on the resolution.

> **Note**
>
> *Usually resolutions are between 640x480 and 1280x1024 pixels. This depends on the monitor and the graphic map. Web sites are today optimised to 800x600 pixels. Changes arise if you produce Web sites for terminals with smaller displays, like PDAs.*

```
<TABLE BORDER="1" WIDTH="300" HEIGHT="300">
<TR>
<TD>Table: 300x300 pixels</TD>
</TR>
</TABLE>
```

In the above example, width and height are indicated in pixels. No details of the unit of measurement are required for this. Pixels are fixed values. If you change the size of the browser window, the table will always stay the same size (Figure 7.2).

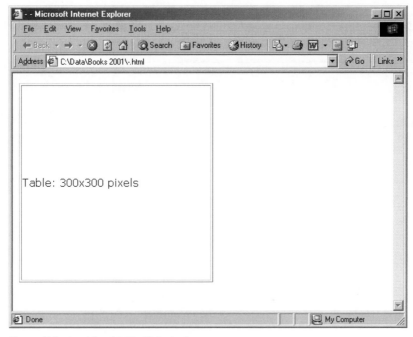

Figure 7.2: A table of 300x300 pixels

With percentages, tables behave a little differently. Here the size of the table depends on the corresponding percentage value of the displayed area in the browser. A % sign is attached to the attributes HEIGHT and WIDTH after the numerical value (Figure 7.3). The following code will give a table that is half the width and half the height of the screen.

```
<TABLE BORDER="1" WIDTH="50%" HEIGHT="50%">
<TR>
<TD>Table: 50%x50% </TD>
</TR>
</TABLE>
```

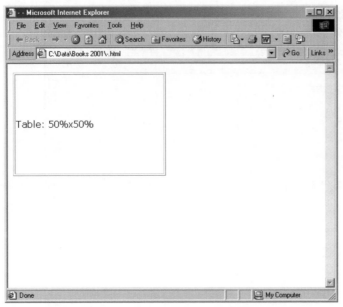

Figure 7.3: A table with the size 50%x50% of the screen size

Rows and cells

The size of the rows and individual cells are all indicated in pixels and percentages. The two attributes WIDTH and HEIGHT come into use here.

In order not to mix up the sizes of rows and cells with each other, there are some simple principles:

- The width of a row always corresponds to the width of the table, which is why only it makes sense to use the HEIGHT attribute in the <TR> tag for the height of the columns.

- The width of a cell indicates the width of the column that goes with it. A column is always displayed as the same width as the widest cell in the column.

- The height of the highest cell determines the height of the whole row. A bigger value than this should not be given for this in the <TR> tag.

This is clarified in the following listing. In this example we have allocated deliberate contradictory values, in order to show which details get preference. In practice, you should of course try to match all values to each other exactly. This means that the sum of the columns should not be wider than the whole table.

> **Caution**
>
> *If you often change the content and size of your table, it can, under these circumstances, result in "bad" calculations and a poor display. Depending on the circumstances, it may be better to create the table first, and only allocate the sizes of the columns at the end of the process.*

```
<TABLE BORDER="1">
<TR HEIGHT="50">
<TH WIDTH="100" HEIGHT="20">Head column 1</TH>
<TH>Head column 2</TH>
</TR>
<TR>
<TD WIDTH="50" HEIGHT="50">Cell 1</TD>
<TD WIDTH="100" HEIGHT="100">Cell 2</TD>
</TR>
</TABLE>
```

[handwritten annotations: "TABLE ROW", "TABLE HEAD", "Try", "Write & check"]

> **Note**
>
> *In the example above, we only use pixel values. This process also works with percentage values of course.*

In the following we go through the listing step by step. The result is seen in Figure 7.4.

1 No size values are indicated in the <TABLE> tag. Where no adjustments in size in the rows or cells follow, the size of the table would be orientated to the content.

2 The first row has a height of 50 pixels. This value is bigger than the tallest cell in the line (20 pixels). The content of the row is also no bigger than 50 pixels. Therefore the value for the height of the row is used.

3 The first head cell (<TH>) in the first row still contains size values. The height is not obtained as already mentioned, however, as the row was defined as higher than this. The width, on the other hand, is the same for the whole column, as the cell directly below only has a width of 50 pixels <TD WIDTH="50" HEIGHT="50">.

4 The cell in the second row does not have much to report. As mentioned earlier, its width is eclipsed by the one above. On the other hand, the height of the second cell in the line is 100 pixels high.

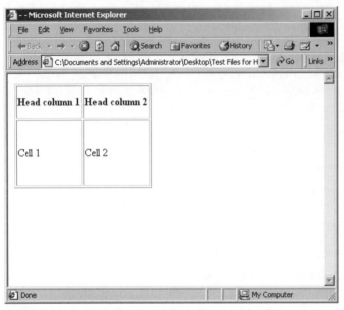

Figure 7.4: Allocating the size of the columns and cells

> **Caution**
>
> *The layout of a table depends, of course, on whether the number of lines, cells, and columns agree. It is best to design a complicated table on paper before you code it. Take care though, as content which is bigger than the size of the cells and the table can destroy your whole layout.*

Formatting tables

This section is about adapting the layout of your table using the attributes in the <TABLE> tag. The basis for the different examples is the following simple HTML table.

```
<TABLE>
```

```
<TR>
<TD>Cell 1</TD>
<TD>Cell 2</TD>
</TR>
<TR>
<TD>Cell 3</TD>
<TD>Cell 4</TD>
</TR>
</TABLE>
```

Frames

We have already introduced the BORDER attribute. It indicates the width of the frame in pixels and is found in the <TABLE> tag. For creative reasons, a frame in not normally used, as it is always displayed in the same way by the browser, which is not always visually pleasing.

> **Tip**
>
> *If you do not allocate a BORDER value but just write the attribute in the*
> *<TABLE> tag, the frame will be one pixel thick.*

In Figure 7.5 you see a simple example. We have indicated a frame of ten pixels in the <TABLE> tag in our example (see previous listing).

```
<TABLE BORDER="10">
```

Figure 7.5: A frame of ten pixels wide

Grids

If you have allocated a width for the BORDER attribute, a grid is also shown automatically in the table. This is one pixel thick by default. To change the width, use the attribute CELLSPACING in the <TABLE> tag (Figure 7.6).

```
<TABLE BORDER="5" CELLSPACING="10">
```

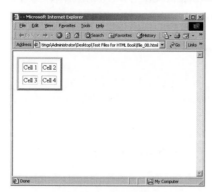

Figure 7.6: The ten pixel grid

For CELLSPACING, a value of one pixel is allocated per default, even if 0 is given as a value for BORDER and the attribute CELLSPACING does not stand in the <TABLE> tag. In order to eliminate the grid lines, you have to allocate CELLSPACING a value of 0 (Figure 7.7).

Figure 7.7: CELLSPACING *of 10 and* BORDER *of 0*

Distance between cell content and cell edge

In the default setting the cell contents are directly (aligned) to the edge of the cell. This doesn't work so well with text. Therefore, in the <TABLE> tag there is the attribute (CELLPADDING.) With this, you can determine the distance between the cell contents and the edge of the cell in pixels.

In the following example we have allocated five pixels for the outer edge, the grid lines, and the distance between the cell contents and the edge of the cell respectively, as follows (Figure 7.8):

```
<TABLE BORDER="5" CELLPADDING="5" CELLSPACING="5">
```

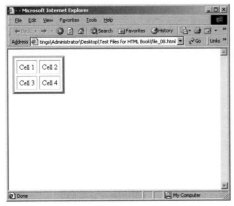

Figure 7.8:The edge, grid, and distance between the cell contents and cell edge are all set at five pixels

Of course, you can also specify a distance between the cell contents and the edge of the cell, if the table contains no edge and no grid. In this case we deal with an invisible table. With CELLPADDING you can control the distance of the individual cell contents from each other. This is double the value of CELLPADDING. If, for example, you want two table cells next to each other between two images to have a distance of ten pixels between them, give a value of five for CELLPADDING (Figure 7.9).

Figure 7.9: In the top table above CELLPADDING *was increased to 5, and* CELLSPACING *to 0, in the lower table above:* CELLPADDING *is changed to 0 and* CELLSPACING *to 5*

Partially showing frames

Since Internet Explorer 4 there has been a new attribute called FRAME. It controls on which side of a table a frame is shown. So that this attribute works, a BORDER must of course be given which must not have the value 0.

> **Caution**
>
> *The attribute FRAME only works with Internet Explorer as from Version 4, not with Netscape Navigator or Opera.*

```
<TABLE FRAME="above" BORDER="0">
```

The above code line shows how to set the frame of the table only at the upper edge of the table. The grid is displayed normally (Figure 7.10).

Figure 7.10: The frame is only shown at the top of the table

Table 7.1 summarises possible values for the FRAME attribute.

Value	Description
above	Only the top frames are visible
below	Only the bottom frames are visible
border	The frames are displayed. Instead of this you can also use the value box or leave out the FRAME attribute
box	The frames are shown completely (see border)
hsides	Only the top and bottom frames are displayed (h is for horizontal).

Value	Description
lhs	Only the frames on the left side of the table are shown (lhs is for left hand side)
rhs	The frames on the right hand side of the table are shown (rhs is for right hand side)
void	No frames are displayed, but the grid lines are visible
vsides	Only the left and right frames are visible (v is for vertical)

Table 7.1: Possible values for the FRAME *attribute*

Also new in Internet Explorer 4 was the attribute RULES for the <TABLE> tag. With this, you determine which parts of the grid are shown.

> **Caution**
>
> *This attribute also only works in Internet Explorer version 4.0 onwards, not in Netscape Navigator or Opera.*

```
<TABLE BORDER="1" RULES="rows">
```

In the above example, using the value rows shows the grid lines between the rows (see Figure 7.11).

Figure 7.11: Grid lines are shown between the rows

The possible values for the RULES attribute are found in Table 7.2.

Value	Description
all	The complete grid is shown. This corresponds to the standard, and is the setting used if the RULES attribute is not put on to the \<TABLE\> tag
cols	The grid is only displayed between the columns and not between the lines
groups	Only certain groups of the table are surrounded with a grid. You will learn more about these groups in the section "Grouping tables"
none	The grid is not shown
rows	Only the grid between the lines, not between the rows, is shown

Table 7.2: Possible values for the RULES attribute

Grouping tables

Internet Explorer (from Version 4 onwards) allows you to subdivide tables into three different areas: table head, body, and foot. You may require these effects if, for example, you want to show only the grid lines for these areas, or if you want to set individual areas with the attribute value RULES="groups" (see above) (Figure 7.12).

> **Caution**
>
> *Grouping tables only works with Internet Explorer version 4 onwards. Netscape Navigator and Opera ignore these tags. Therefore you should only work with them if you know that your users use Internet Explorer (for example in company intranets).*

```
<TABLE BORDER="1" RULES="groups" CELLPADDING="5">
 <THEAD>
  <TR><TD>Head 1</TD><TD>Head 2</TD></TR>
 </THEAD>
 <TBODY>
  <TR><TD>head 1</TD><TD>head 2</TD></TR>
  <TR><TD>Body 3</TD><TD>Body 4</TD></TR>
```

```
</TBODY>

<TFOOT>

 <TR><TD>Foot 1</TD><TD>Foot 2</TD></TR>

</TFOOT>

</TABLE>
```

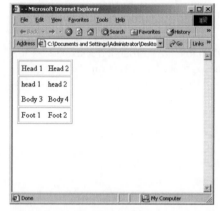

Figure 7.12: A simple grouping

The above example was created in the following way:

1 First, a frame was defined in the `<TABLE>` tag with `BORDER`. Then the attribute `RULES` follows with the value `GROUP`, to show the possible effects of the grouping in different areas. The value `CELLPADDING="5"` is only used for cosmetic reasons, and because of this, the distances between the cells are not small. If `CELLPADDING` and `CELLSPACING` are set to 0, no distance is visible between the cells of an area.

2 In the second step, the table head is defined using the tag `<THEAD>`. It contains all lines that are to be contained in the table head. The table head is completed with `</THEAD>`.

Tip

You can define a background colour or background image for every area. The attribute BGCOLOR *and* BACKGROUND *are used for this. You will learn more about backgrounds in the section of the same name.*

3 The table body is enclosed by the tags <TBODY> and </TBODY>. It can, however, contain many rows.

4 Last, the table foot is set using <TFOOT> and </TFOOT>.

Tip

Several areas can be contained in a table. It is no problem, for example to have two or three table bodies in a table. This is useful if you want to make several areas the same colour.

Background

In this section we show you how to set a background colour for a whole table and table row or cell. At the end you will learn how you can add a background to a table.

Background colours

A background colour is allocated with the attribute BGCOLOR. This attribute is available in both <TABLE>- and in the <TR> and <TD> tag. Values for colours are given either in hexadecimal notation or with the corresponding colour name (possible with 16 colours). A fuller explanation of hexadecimal notation and a list of 16 colours can be found in Chapter 2.

The browser takes into account the background colour of tables, rows and columns in a particular order. The colour of the cell is always first, followed by the colour of the row, then the colour of the table.

147

Note

The colour of the table also determines the colours of the grid in Internet Explorer. In Netscape Navigator, on the other hand, the background colour appears through the grid. In order to set the colour of the frame and the grid in Internet Explorer, use the attribute BORDERCOLOUR *in the* <TABLE> *tag, with which you can define a colour in hexadecimal notation. The Internet Explorer goes a bit further: with* BORDERCOLORDARK *and* BORDERCOLORLIGHT *in the* <TABLE> *tag you set a colour for the dark and bright areas of the frame respectively. Netscape Navigator ignores these attributes.*

Caution

In order to see the background colours in Netscape Navigator the appropriate cells must be filled whether you define a background colour in the <TABLE>, <TR> *or* <TD> *tag or not.*

In the following example we have created a table with three rows and two columns. This is shown in Figure 7.13.

```
<TABLE BORDER="1" CELLPADDING="5" BGCOLOR="red">
<TR>
<TD>Cell 1</TD>
<TD>Cell 2</TD>
</TR>
<TR BGCOLOR="#FFFFFF">
<TD>Cell 3</TD>
<TD>Cell 4</TD>
</TR>
<TR>
<TD BGCOLOR="green">Cell 5</TD>
<TD>Cell 6</TD></TR>
</TABLE>
```

The above example includes the following background colours:

1 The table is made red with `BGCOLOR="red"`.

2 The second row contains the white background colour with
`BGCOLOR="#FFFFF"`.

3 The first cell in the last row is made green by using `BGCOLOR="green"`.

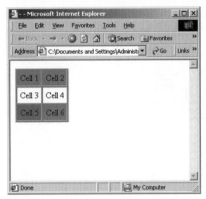

Figure 7.13: A table with several background colours

> **Tip**
>
> *If you allocate a background colour for a table, you should make sure
> the text is displayed in a contrasting colour so that it can be read.*

Using background images

You can set a background image for the whole table. This is done using the
attribute `BACKGROUND`. You already know this as the attribute of the `<BODY>`
tags. Here it assigns a background image to the whole page. If you put this
into the `<TABLE>` tag, the image will only be inserted into the table.

put here background to insert picture into the table

> **Note**
>
> *The attribute `BACKGROUND` for the `<TABLE>` tag does not belong to the
> offical HTML specification, but is supported by all common browsers.*

```
<TABLE WIDTH="500" HEIGHT="300" BORDER="1"
➥BACKGROUND="image.jpg">
```

```
<TR>

<TD>Cell 1</TD>

<TD>Cell 2</TD>

</TR>

</TABLE>
```

The reference to the image is carried out by relative or absolute links. In our example we have created a relative link to an image called `image.jpg` in the folder *images* (Figure 7.14).

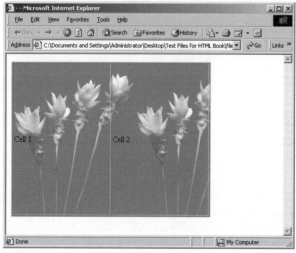

Figure 7.14: Adding a background behind a table

Caution

Netscape Navigator, unlike Internet Explorer and Opera, cuts off the image at the end of the cell (see Figure 7.15). This can be very annoying if you want to spread it over the whole table. It is best to nest two tables into one another, where the outer one contains the image, to prevent this from happening (see Chapter 8).

Figure 7.15: Netscape Navigator cuts off the image at the end of the cell!

Text in a table

Text in a table is formatted in the same way as text outside a table. The only difference is that formatting for every table cell must be carried out individually.

```
<TABLE BORDER="1">

<TR>

<TD>

<FONT FACE="Arial" SIZE="4"><I>Text in Arial, Text grade 4,
➥italic</I></FONT>

</TD>

<TD>

<FONT FACE="Courier" SIZE="2"><B>Text in Courier, Text grade
➥2, bold</B>

</FONT>

</TD>

</TR>

</TABLE>
```

The example above shows that every cell should be formatted individually:

1 In the left hand table cells we have displayed text with the help of the `<FONT>` and `<I>` tag in Arial in text size 4 and italic.

2 In the right hand table cell the `<FONT>` and `<B>` tags are used to display the text in bold Courier with a text size of 2 (Figure 7.16).

Figure 7.16: Different text formatting in a table

Caution

Many HTML editiors put a `<FONT>` tag around the whole table when formatting text. This is only supported by Internet Explorer, not Netscape Navigator. You should therefore use stylesheets instead (see Chapter 10, Stylesheets).

Chapter 8

Tables II

In this chapter we go into more detail on the main functions from the previous chapter. We show you how you can line up tables and cells, connect cells, and use invisible tables, and end with how to nest tables.

Aligning tables

In this section we show you how to align tables and their content.

The ALIGN attribute in the <TABLE> tag is used to align a table on the page.

> **Note**
>
> *The ALIGN attribute in the <TABLE> tag is no longer indicated in the HTML specification, but is supported by all browsers. There are several other options, for example the <CENTER> tag, to centre the table. Stylesheets are another option.*

In the following example we have aligned a table with one cell to the centre:

```
<TABLE BORDER="1" ALIGN="CENTER">
<TR>
<TD>Cell 1</TD>
</TR>
</TABLE>
```

To centre-align the table, the ALIGN attribute with the value CENTER in the <TABLE> tag can be used (Figure 8.1).

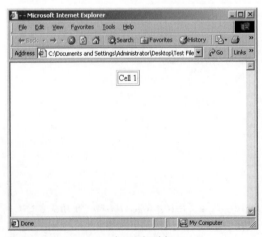

Figure 8.1: A centre-aligned table

As well as CENTER, ALIGN can take on other values which we have summarised in Table 8.1.

Value of ALIGN	Description
CENTER	Table is aligned to the centre
LEFT	Table is aligned to the left of the screen; text is shown to the left of the table
RIGHT	Table is aligned to the right of the edge of the screen; text is aligned to the right of the table

Table 8.1: The value of ALIGN in tables

> **Note**
>
> *A table can only be aligned horizontally. To align it vertically you have to nest two tables in one another. The outer table has a height and width of 100% and a single cell with a vertical alignment to the centre or the bottom edge. The cell which is to be horizontally aligned is contained in this.*

Aligning cell contents

Use the ALIGN attribute to align the cell contents horizontally. For vertical alignment the VALIGN attribute is used (VALIGN, for vertical align). Both attributes have their place in the <TD> tag.

> **Note**
>
> *Head cells are centre-aligned by default (<TH> tag),if they aren't allocated an ALIGN attribute. Normal cells (<TD> tag) are justified to the left. The default for the vertical alignment is, in both cases, the centre.*

> **Tip**
>
> *If you give a value to the ALIGN and VALIGN attributes in the <TR> tag, all cells in this row are aligned according to this. Alignment always has priority in a <TD> tag, however.*

```
<TABLE BORDER="1" WIDTH="100" HEIGHT="100">
<TR>
<TD ALIGN="CENTER" VALIGN="MIDDLE">Cell 1</TD>
</TR>
</TABLE>
```

The following steps are necessary for centre alignment (Figure 8.2):

1 First the table contents are aligned to the centre with `ALIGN="CENTER"`.

2 Following this, `VALIGN="MIDDLE"` is used for vertical centre alignment.

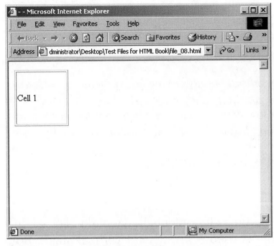

Figure 8.2: Centre aligning cell content.

As well as centre alignment there are other values for the attributes `ALIGN` and `VALIGN` in the `<TD>` tag which we have summarised in Tables 8.2 and 8.3.

Value of `ALIGN`	Description
CENTRE	The cell contents are centre-aligned
LEFT	The cell contents are left-aligned
RIGHT	The cell contents are right-aligned

Table 8.2: The values for `ALIGN` for a table cell

Value of VALIGN	Description
BASELINE	The text rows are aligned so that the uppermost row of text is on the lowest possible line
BOTTOM	The cell content is aligned to the bottom edge of the cell
MIDDLE	The cell content is aligned to the middle. This is the default value
TOP	The cell content is aligned to the top edge of the cell

Table 8.3: The values of VALIGN for a table cell

Creating space between tables

If you want to create another table or image next to, above, or underneath another table, it is often necessary for visual reasons to ensure there is a certain space between the tables. This is done using the attributes HSPACE and VSPACE in the <TABLE> tag. Here you need to indicate a horizontal or vertical distance in pixels.

The horizontal distance with HSPACE is only valid if you have aligned the table with ALIGN left or right, as otherwise no object can be inserted next to the table.

Caution

HSPACE *and* VSPACE *only work in Netscape Navigator, not in Internet Explorer or in Opera. Therefore they are not used very often in practice. Invisible tables are used more often.*

In the following example we have created a distance between a simple table and the text written around it.

```
<HTML>
<HEAD>
<TITLE>Figure 8.3</TITLE>
</HEAD>
<BODY>
Text in front of the table.
```

157

```
<TABLE BORDER="1" WIDTH="100" HEIGHT="100" HSPACE="20"
➥VSPACE="20" ALIGN="LEFT">

<TR>

<TD>Cell 1</TD>

</TR>

</TABLE>

<BR><BR>

Text outside the table.

</BODY>

</HTML>
```

The following steps are necessary to carry out the above example:

1 First insert some text directly after the <BODY> tag.

> **Note**
>
> *Normally, text is inserted into a paragraph, in a <P> tag. We have refrained from doing this here, as the <P> tag inserts a distance after a paragraph which would be joined by VSPACE for effect. We want to show the effect of using VSPACE by itself.*

2 Then create a simple table with one cell. In the <TABLE> tag we have defined the size and the frames of the table.

3 After the table we insert some more text. We create space above it with two line breaks (<BR>).

4 It is particularly important that the table is aligned in the <TABLE> tag with ALIGN="LEFT". With this, the text which was inserted under the table in the HTML document flows on the right of the table as this does not cover the whole screen.

5 The last step is to set another distance to the text above (VSPACE) and next to (HSPACE) of the table (Figure 8.3).

Figure 8.3: Text at a defined distance around the table

Connecting cells

In this section we show you how you can connect several cells. This increases table options.

Connecting cells over rows

The attribute ROWSPAN connects several cells over lines. It can stand in the <TH> or the <TD> tag. The <TH> or the <TD> tag cannot be entered in the connected cells now.

This is illustrated in the following example:

```
<TABLE BORDER="1" WIDTH="150" HEIGHT="100">

<TR>

<TD ROWSPAN="2"><B>Pop stars</B></TD>

<TD>Madonna</TD>

</TR>

<TR>

<TD>Britney Spears</TD>

</TR>

</TABLE>
```

In order to make the above example real (see Figure 8.4), the following steps are necessary:

1 For visual reasons, allocate a frame and a size for the table in the <TABLE> tag.

2 Now we are aiming to extend the first cell over two rows. In order to achieve this, insert the attribute ROWSPAN into the first cell (<TD> tag) and give it the value of 2. This means that this cell connects two rows.

3 The second cell in the first row is then completed using the name of a pop star.

4 The second row only contains one more cell because the first cell from the first row extends to the second row, thanks to ROWSPAN.

Figure 8.4: ROWSPAN *in action*

Connecting cells over columns

To connect cells over several columns, use the attribute COLSPAN in the <TH> or <TD> tag.

```
<TABLE BORDER="1" WIDTH="200" HEIGHT="100">
<TR>
<TD COLSPAN="2" ALIGN="CENTER">
<B>Latin Pop stars</B>
```

160

```
</TD>
</TR>
<TR>
<TD>Jennifer Lopez</TD>
<TD>Ricky Martin</TD>
</TR>
</TABLE>
```

This example works like that of ROWSPAN:

1 First in the row is size and the width of the table frame.

2 Next create a cell in the first row with COLSPAN="2". This means that this cell spans two columns. Because our table will only consist of two columns, do not insert any more cells in the first row.

3 For visual reasons we have displayed the text Latin Pop stars in bold in the cell and we have also centre-aligned it with ALIGN="CENTER".

4 Next you have to create the second row. This consists of two cells (Figure 8.5).

Note

If your table becomes more complicated, draw an outline first. The most common cause of errors in the connection of cells is that cells are actually connected, but are still have a <TD> tag. This superfluous tag is then interpreted as a new cell. You can see an example of this in Figure 8.6. In the top cells we have inserted another cell despite COLSPAN="2". *In the bottom row there only two cells, however. Therefore the eqivalent row for the top cell is missing in the second cell.*

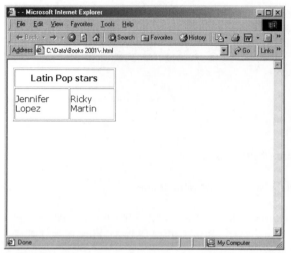

Figure 8.5: Cells from two columns were combined into one

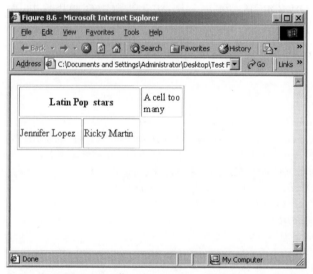

Figure 8.6: An extra cell in the top row of a table

Connecting cells over rows and columns

Of course, COLSPAN and ROWSPAN can also be combined. For this we have designed a complex example. The basis for this is the world map which we used in Chapter 6. We have added to the map some arrows using Photoshop (Figure 8.7).

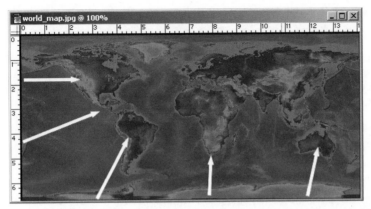

Figure 8.7: The map with arrows in Photoshop

In HTML this example consists of a table with three rows and four columns.

```
<TABLE BORDER="1">
 <TR>
  <TD>North America</TD>
  <TD COLSPAN="3" ROWSPAN="2">
   <IMG SRC="world_map.jpg" WIDTH="532" HEIGHT="252">
  </TD>
 </TR>
 <TR>
  <TD>Central America</TD>
 </TR>
 <TR>
  <TD> </TD>
  <TD ALIGN="CENTER">South America</TD>
  <TD ALIGN="CENTER">South Africa</TD>
  <TD ALIGN="CENTER">Australia</TD>
 </TR>
</TABLE>
```

At the first glance the above code looks more complicated than is actually is:

1 The table consists of three rows and four columns (see Figure 8.8).

2 In the first row the first cell contains North America. This cell in our table is in the top left.

3 The second cell in the first row is important: it contains the image world_map.jpg from the folder *images* and spans over two rows and three columns. The cell is connected to the row below with ROWSPAN and with the two columns with COLSPAN.

4 The second row consists only of the first cell containing Central America. The connected cell in the first row keeps the rest for itself.

5 The third row contains all four cells, three of which contain labels.

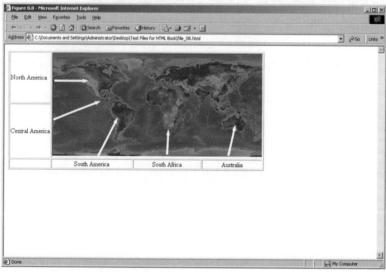

Figure 8.8: The world map labelled

Invisible tables

Invisible tables are mainly used as layout elements. With these you can place objects anywhere you want on the page.

An invisible table has a BORDER of 0 or does not use a BORDER attribute at all. The placement and size of the table parts can be controlled by the attributes WIDTH and HEIGHT or with transparent GIF files. These transparent images must be only 1x1 pixels big so they can be made smaller or bigger with WIDTH and HEIGHT.

In the following, we show you both options using a simple example. The aim is to place an image 200 pixels away from the left and from the top edge of the screen (Figure 8.9).

> **Tip**
>
> *Invisible tables are not only suitable for placing. With the attribute* `BGCOLOR` *you can, for example, create a colour area or set a background colour for text, so that you cannot see the table behind it.*

1 The basis of both options is a table with four cells.

```
<TABLE>
  <TR>
    <TD></TD>
    <TD></TD>
  </TR>
  <TR>
    <TD></TD>
    <TD></TD>
  </TR>
</TABLE>
```

2 Next, insert a cell in the table on the right underneath the image. In our case the name of the image is *image.jpg* and is found in the folder *images*.

```
<TD>
<IMG SRC="images/image.jpg" WIDTH="350" HEIGHT="231">
</TD>
```

3 Now you can control the size of the top left cells with the attribute `WIDTH` and `HEIGHT`. To do so, automatically place the cell on the bottom right of the image.

```
<TABLE>
  <TR>
    <TD WIDTH="200" HEIGHT="200"></TD>
    <TD></TD>
  </TR>
```

```
<TR>

  <TD></TD>

  <TD><IMG SRC="images/image.jpg" WIDTH="350" HEIGHT="231">
➥</TD>

 </TR>

</TABLE>
```

Alternatively you can also insert a 1x1 pixel transparent GIF (*point.gif*) and scale this with WIDTH and HEIGHT to the right size. In this example you can place the transparent GIF either in the top left or top right respectively under a GIF file. We have chosen this option here. By doing so the top right cell is free.

```
<TABLE>

 <TR>

  <TD></TD>

  <TD><IMG SRC="images/point.gif" WIDTH="1" HEIGHT="200">
➥</TD>

 </TR>

 <TR>

  <TD><IMG SRC="images/point.gif" WIDTH="200" HEIGHT="1">
➥</TD>

  <TD><IMG SRC="images/image.jpg" WIDTH="350" HEIGHT="231">
➥</TD>

 </TR>

</TABLE>
```

Figure 8.9: The file was placed 200 pixels from the top and from the left edge of the screen

> **Note**
>
> *In this example the distance from the top edge seems quite a lot bigger. This is the default browser setting, which always inserts a bigger distance from the top edge of the window than the page. The distance is also bigger than the 200 pixels because a slight* CELLSPACING *or* CELLPADDING *is still provided as a default.*

Ordering text in columns

Visible tables are used to allow text to flow in columns. For this a table is used with different cells in a row. With the attribute WIDTH in the <TD> tag you can control the width of the individual columns. With CELLSPACING you can control the distance between the cells. With VALIGN you can align the text vertically. This is best carried out for the whole row in the <TR> tag.

```
<TABLE WIDTH="75%" CELLSPACING="5">

 <TR VALIGN="TOP">

  <TD>Any flowing;text in column 1. Type in the text here.
➥</TD>
```

```
    <TD>Any flowing;text in column 2. You can also insert the
➥image here.</TD>

    <TD>Any flowing text in column 3. Your  text follows
➥here.</TD>

    <TD>Any flowing text in column 4, follows from some
➥text.</TD>

  </TR>

</TABLE>
```

To program the above example (see Figure 8.10) the following steps are necessary:

1 First you must create a table with four cells.

2 Next you specify a width for the table with `WIDTH`.

> **Note**
>
> *If you have not specified a width for the cells and these only contain text and no pictures, all cells are displayed the same size, and it is possible that a column may contain an element (word or image) that is bigger than the optimal column width.*

3 You can control the distance between the cells and between the text in the columns with `CELLSPACING`.

4 You can align all the cell contents of the row to the top edge with `VALIGN="TOP"` in the `<TR>` tag.

5 Last, you must only enter text in the four cells.

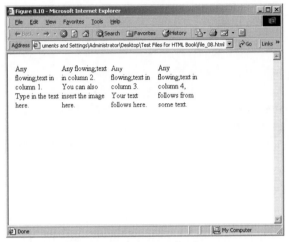

Figure 8.10: Text flowing in several columns

Nesting tables ← one into another

Tables can be nested in each other. In order to do so, you simply insert a table into a cell of another table.

What can you do with tables that have been nested? In principle you can accomplish any layout task. Normally, a large table is used which is first structured. Other tables are then contained within this.

A simple example of this is a Navigations list on the left-hand side of the page to the left of a picture. The following steps are necessary:

1 First create a table consisting of two cells. In the left cell is the navigations list, in the right is the page content.

```
<TABLE CELLPADDING="0" CELLSPACING="0" WIDTH="100%">
 <TR>
  <TD></TD>
  <TD></TD>
 </TR>
</TABLE>
```

2 You should carry out the following adjustments in the <TABLE> tag:

- CELLPADDING and CELLSPACING are set to 0, so that there is no distance between the cells in the large table.

169

- The width of the table is fixed to 100% with the attribute WIDTH of the window.

3 Set the width of the left-hand cell to 100 pixels, and align it vertically to the top edge in the <TD> tag of the table.

```
<TD WIDTH="100" VALIGN="TOP">
```

4 Insert the image into the right-hand cell. We have chosen the file *world.gif* from the directory *images*.

```
<TD><IMG SRC="images/world.gif" WIDTH="532" HEIGHT="252"></TD>
```

5 In the next step you have to insert a table for the navigation elements in the left-hand cell of the large table. This consists of as many rows as you need for navigation points. In the example the four rows each have one cell.

```
<TABLE>
 <TR>
  <TD></TD>
 </TR>
 <TR>
  <TD></TD>
 </TR>
 <TR>
  <TD></TD>
 </TR>
 <TR>
  <TD></TD>
 </TR>
</TABLE>
```

6 Now insert the navigation points into the cells of the table just made (Figure 8.11).

```
<TABLE CELLPADDING="0" CELLSPACING="0" WIDTH="100%">
 <TR>
  <TD WIDTH="100" VALIGN="TOP">
  <TABLE>
    <TR>
     <TD><A HREF="home.htm">Home</A></TD>
    </TR>
    <TR>
     <TD>Product</TD>
    </TR>
    <TR>
     <TD>Team</TD>
    </TR>
    <TR>
     <TD>contact</TD>
    </TR>
  </TABLE></TD>
  <TD><IMG SRC="images/world.gif" WIDTH="532"
          HEIGHT="252"></TD>
 </TR>
</TABLE>
```

Figure 8.11: The finished page

Chapter 9

Forms

*Forms are used by many operators of Web sites to obtain feedback.
Both parties profit from this: The user can indicate in a structured
and specific way, what's bothering him and what he really wants
to be rid of. The site operator, in turn, gets feedback in a format
that he can analyse easily, and he can, using skilful form design,
indicate all of the important details (eg. e-mail address) he needs
to know about the surfer. In this chapter we show you how to
create this kind of form in HTML. Then, we show you how the
data from the form can be sent by e-mail.*

Motivation

As already mentioned in the Introduction, forms frequently appear on the World Wide Web. There are several uses for these forms which we will now demonstrate using examples from the World Wide Web:

- **Feedback/Re-registration** to the operator of the Web site. In general, the user can give data such as names, email addresses, and his own requests. Manufacturers support can also be dealt with more effectively using these forms than purely by email, as all important data can be eliminated (see Figure 9.1).

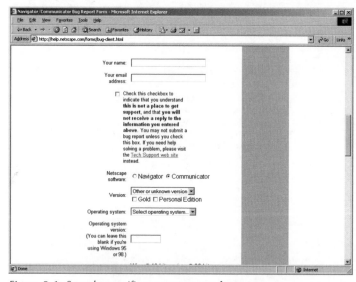

Figure 9.1: Sample-specific support query form

- **Surveys**. Many people find the Internet economical. What can be more reasonable then, than to conduct a survey? As a rule, in a survey a whole load of questions are asked, which can be answered by typing a response in, or by choosing one of several answers (multiple choice).

In Figure 9.2 you can see an excerpt of a survey conducted by internet Survey. Under www.internetsurvey.co.uk, you can regularly find the biggest survey about the Internet in Europe. In addition, you can also find the most important results of the survey, so a visit is always worth while!

interesting page

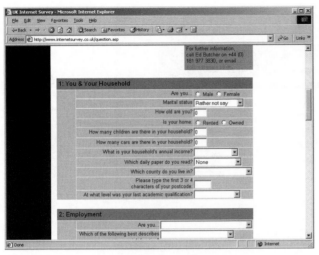

Figure 9.2: Internet survey has lots of forms

- **Navigation**. A possible element of the form, is a drop down menu. In this kind of menu there are several entries from which you can choose one (or several). This usually executes an action such as loading another Web site. In Figure 9.3 you can see that, within a support area in the software, updates for a particular product can be selected. The name of the product should not be typed in, but rather selected from the drop down menu (first the product group, then the product family, then the product). Figure 9.4 shows a format currently popular on Web pages: In a drop down menu you can find the most important areas of a Web site executed. After selecting one of these areas they are loaded directly into the browser.

Figure 9.3: Choice of products with a form

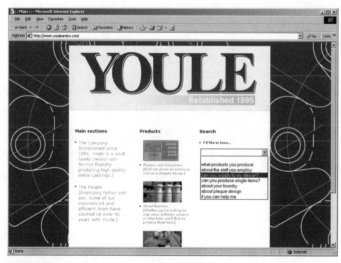

Figure 9.4: Fast navigation with a drop down menu

- **Text output.** By using JavaScript, a programming language embedded in HTML, you can control the content of the form elements. This is illustrated in Figure 9.5 which shows how a SMS can be sent: A short message can only have 160 characters (as you see in the figure, many operators allow even fewer, so they can fill the rest of the SMS with adverts). In the background the number of characters that are available is shown. This is indicated in the text input field.

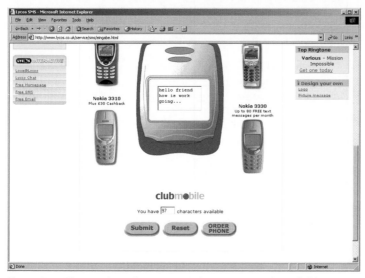

Figure 9.5: The number of remaining characters in a form field

In principle only one of these possibilities can be put into effect with pure HTML. This is feedback. First, however, we must look at the principle construction of a form, and then at the individual elements that a form can contain.

Form frames

Forms are surrounded by the tag `<FORM>` as follows:

```
<FORM>
<!-- Form elements -->
</FORM>
```

177

The `<FORM>` tag has several interesting attributes which will be covered in this chapter. For the sake of clarity we will introduce them here (Table 9.1) and return to them later:

Attribute	Description	Default value, if not indicated
ACTION	The Web site indicates the form data to be sent. For example, a program on the server that forwards the form details.	the current page
ENCTYPE	Files can also be sent with a form. In doing this, the closing type must be indicated. This value is also important when sending things by email.	text/www-url-encoded
METHOD	Method of sending, either GET or POST	GET

Table 9.1: Attributes of the `<FORM>` tag

Form elements

We will now look at different form elements.

Text fields

Text fields are possibly the most frequently used form fields on the Web. They can be used, among other things, for the following purposes:

- Details of forename, surname and address
- Input of order quantities
- One line of text.

A text field looks like this:

```
<INPUT TYPE="TEXT"
        NAME="Name"
        VALUE="Value"
        SIZE="Length"
```

```
MAXLENGTH="Maximum length">
```

The individual parameters:

- TYPE="TEXT" – identifies the form element as a text field. It is also the default, and can be left out.

- NAME – an obvious identifier for the form field. It is important for sending information (see below), so it is therefore an obligatory detail.

- VALUE – the value with which the field is filled. Optional.

- SIZE – length of the field in characters. The length only indicates what is shown; otherwise a lot of characters are entered in the text field, (almost) without limit. Optional.

- MAXLENGTH – Maximum number of characters which can be entered in the text field. Optional.

The following form demonstrates the effect of these details. Make sure that all form fields are filled by using the VALUE attribute, so that you can see the effects of the parameter straight away. Note, however, that you would not normally do this.

```
<FORM>
Forename: <INPUT TYPE="TEXT" SIZE="8"
                VALUE="CHRISTIAN"><BR>
Surname: <INPUT TYPE="TEXT" SIZE="8"
                VALUE="WENZ"><BR>
Book title: <INPUT TYPE="TEXT" SIZE="10"
                MAXLENGTH="8">
</FORM>
```

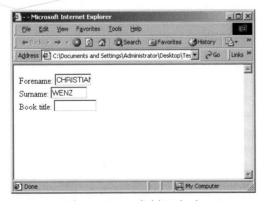

Figure 9.6: The text input field in the browser

In Figure 9.6 you can see the following:

- The width of the text input field varies according to the chosen type face. The value is not representative of a proportional type face because eight i's take up less space than eight o's.

- SIZE gives the actual width of the display in the text field; more characters can be entered here than are shown in the field.

- MAXLENGTH reduces the number of characters which can be inputted. Therefore, try, to input "HTML EASY" in the third input field...

Password fields

Password fields, as the name suggests, are used for the input of passwords, be it Web mail login, on-line banking, or accessing secure areas of a Web site.

The password fields are constructed syntactically similarly to text input fields:

```
<INPUT TYPE="PASSWORD"
        NAME="Name"
        VALUE="Value"
        SIZE="Length"
        MAXLENGTH="Maximumlength"

>
```

There is one main difference in the parameters for password fields: In the value attribute the characters are indicated with a series of asterisks to preserve the element of secrecy. Let's take a look at the parameters:

- TYPE="PASSWORD" – labels the form element as a password field, and is an obligatory detail.
- NAME – clear identifier for the form field. Obligatory.
- VALUE – the value with which the field is filled. In the display a star indicates a character, in the VALUE attribute there must be plain text. Optional.
- SIZE – Field length in characters. This does not simply refer to the length of the display, as more characters can be written in the field itself. Optional.
- MAXLENGTH – Maximum number of characters which can be entered in the password field. Optional detail.

Here is how to construct a sample form as shown in Figure 9.7:

```
<FORM>
Password 1: <INPUT TYPE="PASSWORD" SIZE="8"
               VALUE="secret"><BR>
Password 2: <INPUT TYPE="PASSWORD" SIZE="8">
</FORM>
```

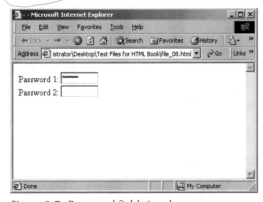

Figure 9.7: Password fields in a browser

You can see that stars are displayed instead of characters. If you type in text in the second password field, stars are shown as well.

Multi-row text fields

A multi-row text field is similar to a single line text field, only several lines are available. They are used for the following:

- Comments in feedback forms
- Entries in guest books
- Longer texts that would not be completely readable in a one line text field.

Syntax:

```
<TEXTAREA NAME="Name"
          ROWS="rows"
          COLS="columns"
          WRAP="breakart"
>Text</TEXTAREA>
```

The parameters for multi-row text text fields are complex:

- NAME – obvious identifier for the text field. Obligatory.
- ROWS – gives the number of rows in the text field. This is limited only by the input. As soon as more rows are indicated scroll bars appear. Obligatory.
- COLS – gives the number of characters per row in the text field. This is only limited to the input. As soon as more rows are indicated, the browser breaks it up or scroll bars appear. Obligatory.
- WRAP – A kind of break. Possible values are: "off" (no row breaks, default setting of Netscape Navigator), "virtual" (automatic break in the display, default setting of Internet Explorer) and "physical" (automatic break, the breaks are kept when the form is sent). This detail is optional, but as a rule "virtual" is a must.
- Text – The text with which the field is filled. HTML must be coded, < instead of < etc. Row breaks are kept, however.

The size of the input in a text field is restricted for the most part by the browser. 16 bit versions of Netscape Navigator are limited to 32 KB (32,768 characters). Today even more characters are possible, though only a few use so many. We can create the multi row text field on Figure 9.8 by using the following syntax:

```
<FORM>
Your opinion, please!
<TEXTAREA NAME="Comments"
          ROWS="8"
          COLS="50"
          WRAP="VIRTUAL"
>
Man is a limited being. Sundays are devoted to
reconsidering our restrictions. It is material
sufferings that we barely notice during the frenzy
of the week, so we immediately consult the doctor.
If our restrictions are economic and even civic,
so our  professionals are required to observe their
agenda. If that which plagues us is intellectual or
moral, so we have a friend, a confidante to whom to
turn, and whose advice and influence to seek: enough,
that is the law: nobody may prolong a worry or
grievance into the new week.
</TEXTAREA>
</FORM>
```

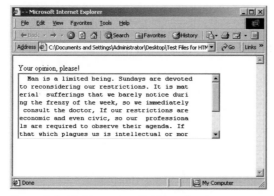

Figure 9.8: Multi-row text field in a browser

If you change WRAP="VIRTUAL" to WRAP="OFF" you have to scroll a great deal, as shown in Figure 9.9.

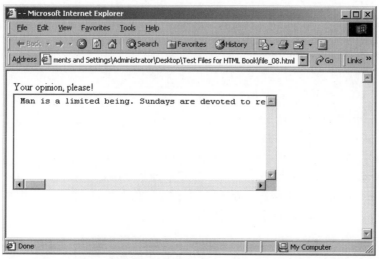

Figure 9.9: No break in Internet Explorer

Check boxes

Check boxes or control fields are small boxes which only have two conditions: On and off (see Figure 9.10). Depending on the operating system and the browser, an active check box is labelled through a hooklet or cross, or another graphic. Here are some areas of use for checkboxes:

- "Yes, I have read your terms and conditions and accept them."

- "No, I do not want to receive any advertisements from you by email."

- In questions for which there are several possible answers ("What hobbies do you have?"), every possible answer is displayed in a check box.

Syntax:

```
<INPUT TYPE="CHECKBOX"
       NAME="Name"
       VALUE="value"
       CHECKED
>
```

Here is an overview of the parameters:

- TYPE="CHECKBOX" – identifies the form element as a check box. Obligatory.

- NAME – obvious identifier for the check box. Obligatory.

- VALUE – value of the check box. This is submitted when the form is sent, as long as the check box is marked with a cross. If no value is indicated, "on" is used as the default. Optional.

- CHECKED – this is only indicated if the check box is marked with a cross from the outset. *poczotek*

```
<FORM>
Which writers do you read?<BR>
Goethe
   <INPUT TYPE="CHECKBOX" NAME="Goethe"
        CHECKED><BR>
Schiller
   <INPUT TYPE="CHECKBOX" NAME="Schiller"
        CHECKED><BR>
Kleist
   <INPUT TYPE="CHECKBOX" NAME="Kleist"
        CHECKED><BR>
Rowling
   <INPUT TYPE="CHECKBOX" NAME="Rowling">
</FORM>
```

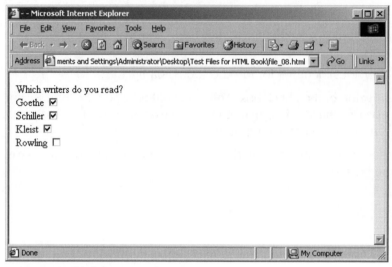

Figure 9.10: Check boxes in a browser

Radio buttons

Radio buttons, like check boxes have only two conditions: active and inactive. In contrast to check boxes, radio buttons always appear in packs. This means that several of them are combined in one group (see Figure 9.11). Of all the radio buttons in a group, only one can be activated at a time. If another one is clicked on, the previous button becomes inactive.

In practice, radio buttons are used for the following:

- Sex: male/female
- Choice between private and company address
- Questions with several possible answers from which only one can be chosen.

The syntax of a radio button looks like this:

```
<INPUT TYPE="RADIO"
       NAME="Name"
       VALUE="value"
       CHECKED
>
```

The following parameters are available:

- TYPE="RADIO" – indicates the form element as a radio button. Obligatory.

- NAME – obvious identifier of the group of radio buttons. Obligatory.

- VALUE – value of the radio buttons, distinguishing criteria within a group from radio buttons. Obligatory.

- CHECKED – This is only indicated if the radio button is pre-selected. Optional.

Inside the group of radio buttons, the VALUE attribute distinguishes each of the values from one another. In the example below you can see how best to select the name for the attribute: NAME for the generic term, VALUE for the individual sub terms.

```
<FORM>
Sex:<BR>
<INPUT TYPE="RADIO" NAME="Sex"
      VALUE="m">male |
<INPUT TYPE="RADIO" NAME="Sex"
      VALUE="f">female<BR>
Your favourite writer:<BR>
<INPUT TYPE="RADIO" NAME="Writer"
      VALUE="Goethe">Goethe |
<INPUT TYPE="RADIO" NAME="Writer"
      VALUE="Schiller">Schiller |
<INPUT TYPE="RADIO" NAME="Writer"
      VALUE="Kleist">Kleist |
<INPUT TYPE="RADIO" NAME="Writer"
      VALUE="Rowling" CHECKED>Rowling
</FORM>
```

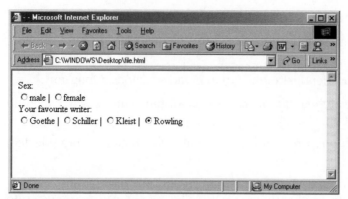

Figure 9.11: Radio buttons in the browser

Type in the example, load this onto your Web browser, and watch what happens if you activate a different radio button than the one which has been selected already.

Drop-down menus

Drop-down menus, or roll-up menus, offer the user several choices. Depending on the type of drop-down menu, the user can choose one or more of the alternatives. Areas of use are, among other things:

- Sex: male/female

- Choice between private and company address

- Questions with several possible answers from which one or more can be chosen.

Here is a new tag, `<SELECT>`. The syntax is as follows:

```
<SELECT NAME="Name"
        SIZE="size"
        MULTIPLE
>
...
</SELECT>
```

Explanations of the individual attributes:

- NAME – obvious identifier of the drop-down menu. Obligatory.

- SIZE – indicates how many elements in the menu can be shown at the same time. The default value is 1. Optional.

- MULTIPLE – If this is indicated, several elements can be selected from the list. Otherwise, only one can be. Optional.

The individual options stand inside of the <SELECT> element. There is a new tag for this: <OPTION>. And the syntax is as follows:

```
<OPTION VALUE="value"
        SELECTED>
  description text
</OPTION>
```

- VALUE – The value which is submitted when the form is sent if the element is selected. If no VALUE attribute is indicated, most browsers take the description text. This is obligatory.

- SELECTED – If this is indicated, the element is pre-selected.

- Description text – The text which is visible in the browser.

In Figure 9.12 you will find two drop-down menus. One of these is a multiple choice selection (MULTIPLE), in which you can also choose additional elements. The syntax is as follows:

```
<FORM>
Sex:
<SELECT NAME="Sex">
  <OPTION VALUE="m">male</OPTION>
  <OPTION VALUE="f">female</OPTION>
</SELECT><BR>
Which writer's books do you like to read?
<SELECT NAME="Writer" SIZE="3" MULTIPLE>
  <OPTION VALUE="Goethe">Goethe</OPTION>
  <OPTION VALUE="Schiller" SELECTED>Schiller
  </OPTION>
  <OPTION VALUE="Kleist" SELECTED>Kleist</OPTION>
  <OPTION VALUE="Rowling">Rowling</OPTION>
```

```
</SELECT>

</FORM>
```

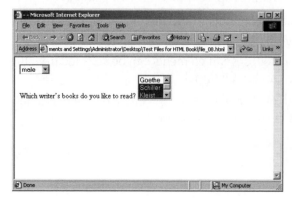

Figure 9.12: Drop-down menu in a browser

> **Note**
>
> *To choose several entries, you have to keep the* Ctrl *key pressed down and click on individual elements.*

File uploads

With HTML, you can offer the user the option of sending files together with the form. If you want to reprocess this file, as a rule, you have to use a server page programming language such as PHP. For this reason, we will only briefly outline the tag here:

```
<INPUT TYPE="FILE"
      NAME="Name"
      MAXLENGTH="Maximumsize"
      SIZE="display length of the input field"
>
```

The individual attributes:

- TYPE="FILE" – identifies the form field as a file upload. Obligatory.

- NAME – Obvious identifier for the form field. Obligatory.

- MAXLENGTH – maximum size for the transferred file in bytes. Optional.

- SIZE – maximum length of the input field in characters (for the display only, otherwise unlimited). Optional.

In Figure 9.13 you can see how the following code might look in the browser:

```
<FORM>
<INPUT TYPE="FILE" NAME="File" SIZE="20">
</FORM>
```

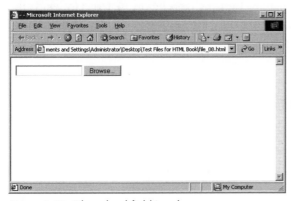

Figure 9.13: File upload field in a browser

By clicking on BROWSER the dialogue box OPEN is revealed. The user can now select the file to be transferred (see Figure 9.14).

Figure 9.14: The dialogue box CHOOSE FILE opens

Invisible fields

In an invisible field, you can send out data which is not shown on the Web site with a form:

```
<INPUT TYPE="HIDDEN"
      NAME="Name"
      VALUE="Value"
>
```

You will find no figure for the listing because the form element, as the name suggests, is not shown in the browser.

Buttons

With HTML you can also display buttons (see Figure 9.15). However the following have no function, and are only interesting in connection with Java Script:

```
<INPUT TYPE="BUTTON"
      NAME="Name"
      VALUE="description"
>
```

The individual attributes are self explanatory.

Here is an example - but be warned: If you click on the button, it won't do anything!

```
<FORM>
<INPUT TYPE="BUTTON" NAME="Test" VALUE="Hello!">
</FORM>
```

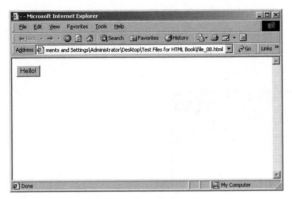

Figure 9.15: Buttons in a browser

We now come to buttons that can actually function!

The Reset button

A reset button is found more and more often on the World Wide Web. With this button, you can undo all of the previous completed entries in a form, and restore it to its initial state (empty or already filled using VALUE attributes).

The syntax of this button is easy:

```
<INPUT TYPE="RESET"
       NAME="Name"
       VALUE="Description"
>
```

The parameters are more complex:

- TYPE="RESET" – identifies the form element as a button. Obligatory.

- NAME – obvious identifier for the form element. It is actually obligatory, but is in practice unnecessary;

- VALUE – description of the button. Optional. If this is left out, the browser assumes the label "reset".

Here is an example. The text input field in Figure 9.16 is already filled with "Goethe". If you change this and then click on the RESET button, the original state is restored ie. the text field is filled with "Goethe" again. the syntax is as follows:

```
<FORM>
Favourite author
```

```
<INPUT TYPE="TEXT" NAME="favourite author"
                   VALUE="Goethe"><BR>
<INPUT TYPE="RESET" VALUE="delete">
</FORM>
```

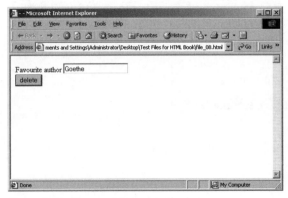

Figure 9.16: The reset button in the browser

The Send button

Finally we come to the most important form element: the button for sending a form. The syntax for Figure 9.17 is as follows:

```
<INPUT TYPE="SUBMIT"
       NAME="Name"
       VALUE="Description"

>
```

The parameters are as those of Reset buttons.

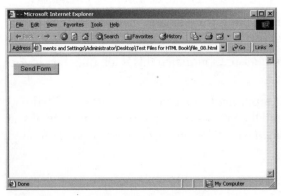

Figure 9.17: The Send button in a browser

Sending forms

You are now in position to create an HTML form. But how will we send it? There are two options, a technically inferior way, which very rarely works as desired, or an advanced way which is very reliable. We will discuss these one at a time.

By email

The most obvious way of sending a form. However, you will need a correctly set up email program. Microsoft and Netscape now offer their own email programs which are more or less integrated into the browser. If these programs are correctly installed *and* the user surfs with the browser which is integrated in the email program, then the email is sent automatically, and for the most part successfully.

> **Caution**
>
> *Another word of warning: In Netscape, this usually works well; in Netscape Explorer up to version 3, it does not; in version 4, it works sometimes; and with version 5, more often than not. It would not be fair of us if this deficit was not made clear!*

To set-up a form so that it can be sent by email (see Figure 9.18), you have to carry out the following steps:

1 Create an HTML form like the ones we have shown.

2 In the <FORM> tag, set the METHOD attribute to "POST".

3 In the <FORM> tag, set the ENCTYPE attribute to "text/plain".

4 In the <FORM> tag, set the ACTION attribute to mailto:your@email address.co.uk.

The syntax for your form is as follows:

```
<FORM ACTION="mailto:paul@cybertechnics.co.uk"
      METHOD="POST" ENCTYPE="text/plain">
Forename: <INPUT TYPE="TEXT" SIZE="8"><BR>
Surname: <INPUT TYPE="TEXT" SIZE="8"><BR>
Sex:<BR>
```

```
<INPUT TYPE="RADIO" NAME="sex"
        VALUE="m">male |
<INPUT TYPE="RADIO" NAME="male"
        VALUE="f">female<BR>
<TEXTAREA NAME="comments"
            ROWS="8"
            COLS="50"
            WRAP="VIRTUAL"
>comments about the book
</TEXTAREA><BR>
Which writer's books do you like to read?
<SELECT NAME="Author" SIZE="4" MULTIPLE>
  <OPTION VALUE="Goethe">Goethe</OPTION>
  <OPTION VALUE="Schiller">Schiller
  </OPTION>
  <OPTION VALUE="Kleist">Kleist</OPTION>
  <OPTION VALUE="Rowling">Rowling</OPTION>
</SELECT><BR>
<INPUT TYPE="CHECKBOX" NAME="OK">
I would like to subscribe to the electronic newsletter.<BR>
<INPUT TYPE="SUBMIT" VALUE="send data">
</FORM>
```

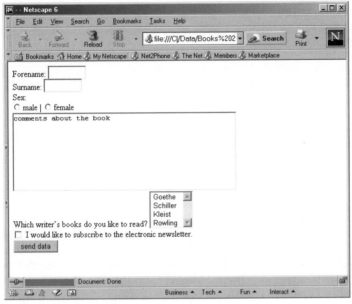

Figure 9.18: The form in a browser

If you want to send the form, the dialogue box which is shown in Figure 9.19 appears. You cannot send a form by this method without showing a dialogue box like this.

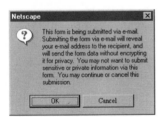

Figure 9.19: This warning message appears before you can send your form

The format in which the details arrive can be seen in Figure 9.20. Here you can see the NAME and the VALUE attributes that go with it, or the values entered.

Subject: Form posted from Mozilla
  Date: Tue, 20 Feb 2001 10:39:00 +0100
  From: paul@cybertechnics.co.uk

Sex = m
Comment = a terrific book.
I say this is quite an objective point of view.

Author = Goethe
Author = Shimmer
Author = Kleist
Ok = on

Figure 9.20: The generated email

Digression: by CGI script

If you want to tackle sending forms in a more professional manner, you have to use so-called CGI script. Unfortunately we do not go into CGI script in this book, and few providers support them. However, on the World Wide Web there are a number of services which enable you to dispatch forms. One of these (free of charge for non-commercial use) is TECHForm, whose Web site is shown in Figure 9.21.

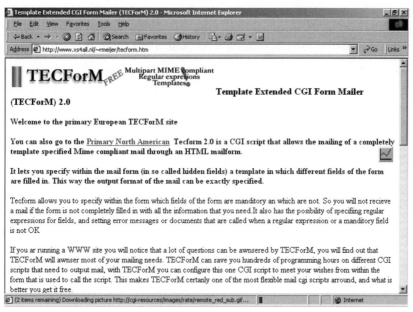

Figure 9.21: The Web site of TECHForm (`www.xs4all.nl/~rmeijer/`
`tecform.htm`*).*

There are other comparable services. However, at this point we do not want to go into these one by one. What we offer is, an approach which works with most of these services in principle. You can find precise step by step instructions on the home page of the provider.

1 The method of sending is always POST (`<FORM METHOD="POST">`).

2 The data type (`<FORM ENCTYPE>`) must not be indicated, `ENCTYPE="multipart/form-data"` is only obligatory for file uploads.

3 Destination (`<FORM ACTION>`) is the provider's own script. It will tell you what this is.

4 You identify yourself to the provider, indicating a particular code, for example your customer number in a concealed form field (see the section Invisible Fields).

5 If you register with the service, your email address will be deposited there, and as soon as a form is sent, it will be evaluated on the Web server of your provider and sent to you by email.

How the data is then processed is up to the provider.

We cannot stress enough that sending by CGI is preferred in all cases as it always works (unless the provider has a server failure). Direct sending by e-mail is prone to faults, and the warning message confuses many surfers.

Chapter 10

Stylesheets

Tags are formatted with stylesheets. The language used for formatting HTML pages is Cascading Stylesheets (CSS). It is this that we shall discuss in Chapter 10, although there are other conventions such as XLS, the stylesheet language for XML. CSS Version 1.0 works with Netscape Navigator from Version 4 onwards and Internet Explorer Version 3. It is therefore, virtually a default. CSS Version 2.0 is the responsibility of the W3C consortium (www.w3c.org) and is now available. It is used for the fourth versions onwards of both Netscape Navigator and Internet Explorer.

Different kinds of stylesheets

Different kinds of stylesheets can be distinguished from each other according to the place at which they are bound. One can assign individual styles of HTML commands, or one can define them at the head of the HTML page. If you want to define a stylesheet globally for several documents, treat it as a file (with the file ending `.css`) and load it in the head of the HTML page.

If you want to use several kinds of stylesheets in one document, there is a clear sequence in which they are used. First, the stylesheet definitions are selected at the top of the HTML page, then the ones at the bottom. If there are different styles for the HTML commands, the top ones are replaced by the bottom ones. The following rules arise from this:

- Styles in HTML commands always overwrite the definitions at the head of the HTML page.

- Stylesheet definitions at the head of the HTML page – whether external or not– always overwrite the previous corresponding definitions if they clash.

Style in the HTML tag

If you define a style in the HTML tag, it is only defined for this tag.

In this example we will establish a style for a paragraph.

```
<P STYLE="color: blue; font-family: Courier">Blue text in
➥Courier</P>
```

This can be created in the following way and is illustrated in Figure 10.1.

1 In the `<P>` tag, define the style for the paragraph with the attribute `STYLE`.

2 First of all, the colour of the text is allocated. The attribute `color:` is used for this. Colour is indicated in either hexadecimal notation or a colour value.

3 The different settings of the style are separated with a semicolon.

4 The second setting is the attribute `font-family: Courier`, which sets the text of the paragraph.

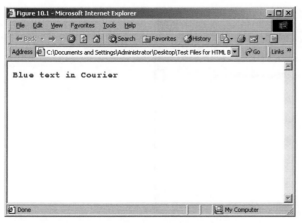

Figure 10.1: A style is defined for the paragraph

If you do not want to define a style for the whole paragraph, for a list, or a table, but want to do so for part of a text, as in Figure 10.2, you must use the tag <SPAN>. Using this, you can determine the style for the area within the tag, as follows:

```
<P>A normal paragraph with
<SPAN STYLE="color: blue; font-family=Courier">blue text in
➥Courier</SPAN>
 in between</P>
```

> **Note**
>
> *If a style had been defined in the <P> tag, this would have been overwritten by the style in the <SPAN> tag as it would have come next in the sequence.*

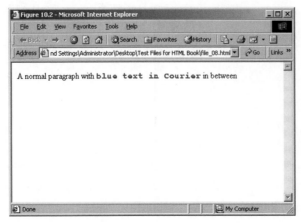

Figure 10.2: A stylesheet definition in the <SPAN> tag

The stylesheet at the head of an HTML page

One of the most important functions of stylesheets is to make it possible to format large areas. Of course this is of no use with style definitions in HTML tags. The overall style of the Web site should be defined at the head of the HTML page. In order to do this you have to insert the tag <STYLE> between <HEAD> and </HEAD>.

The example in Figure 10.3 was created using the following steps:

1 First a stylesheet was defined at the head of the HTML page between <HEAD> and </HEAD>. The <STYLE> tag is used for this.

2 The kind of stylesheet is established with TYPE="text/css". This means that it is a Cascading Stylesheet.

> **Note**
>
> *You can also leave out* TYPE*. Then the browser automatically finds out which kind of stylesheet it is. For accurate programming though, you should always indicate* TYPE*.*

3 A stylesheet definition always begins with the start of a comment `<!--`. In doing so, you prevent older browsers displaying the content of the stylesheet definition incorrectly. The comment is closed with `-->`.

4 With `P` you establish that the style for all `<P>` tags in the HTML page is to be used. The definition is found in curly brackets.

5 We have inserted two paragraphs at the head of the HTML page as an example. Neither have their own style, therefore, the style definition from the head of the HTML page is used (see Figure 10.3).

The syntax should look like this:

```
<HTML>
<HEAD>
 <TITLE>Figure 10.3</TITLE>
 <STYLE TYPE="text/css">
  <!--
  P {color: blue; font-family:Courier}
  -->
 </STYLE>
</HEAD>
<BODY>
 <P>A normal paragraph with blue text in courier.</P>
 <P>Another paragraph with blue text in courier.</P>
</BODY>
</HTML>
```

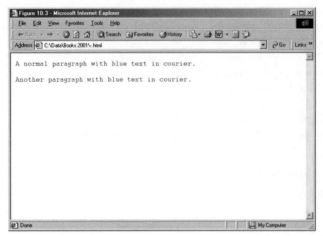

Figure 10.3: Both paragraphs are blue and in courier as the style at the head of the HTML page defines

Importing external stylesheets

If you want to create a large Web site with lots of HTML pages, you will have to define a stylesheet which is not at the top of every HTML page. Instead, create a stylesheet file and import this into every HTML page.

The external stylesheet file is best created with a text or HTML editor. Save the file with using the ending .css.

> **Tip**
>
> *Many HTML editing programs have an in-built function that creates stylesheet files.*

For this example we have called the file `style.css`. It has the following contents:

```
P {color: blue; font-family: Courier}
```

This corresponds exactly to the stylesheet definition at the head of the page. However, the `<STYLE>` tag is discontinued.

In the HTML page, the whole thing looks a bit different: Here, the stylesheet file has to be imported. This takes place in the `<STYLE>` tag at the head of the page.

The syntax is as follows:

```
<HTML>
<HEAD>
 <TITLE>Figure 10.4</TITLE>
 <STYLE TYPE="text/css">
  <!--
  @import url(style.css);
  LI {color: red; font-family: Verdana}
  -->
 </STYLE>
</HEAD>
<BODY>
 <P>A normal paragraph with blue text in courier.</P>
 <P>Another paragraph with blue text in courier.</P>
 <UL>
  <LI>A list in red and verdana.</LI>
 </UL>
</BODY>
</HTML>
```

The following functions apply to the example in Figure 10.4:

1 Within the <STYLE> tag, after the normal comment characters, the command `@import url(style.css)` is used to import the file with the name `style.css`. You can of course insert any kind of link between the brackets of the url.

2 After the import command and the semicolon, you can define any style you want. This only applies for this HTML page. In this example, it is the definition of a colour and type face for the <LI> tag.

3 In the body of the HTML page, we have now created a list and two normal paragraphs. This shows the how stylesheets work (see Figure 10.4).

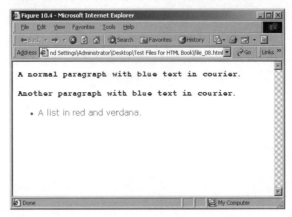

Figure 10.4: Formatting with an imported stylesheet

Linking external stylesheets

If you use a global stylesheet, you can not only import it, but also link to it. In order to do this, the tag <LINK> is used at the head of the relevant HTML page.

Here we use the stylesheet file `style.css` again.

The HTML page to which the external stylesheet is linked looks like this:

```
<HTML>
<HEAD>
 <TITLE>Figure 10.5</TITLE>
 <LINK HREF="style.css" REL=stylesheet TYPE="text/css"
➥TITLE="stylesheet1">
 <STYLE TYPE="text/css">
  <!--
```

```
    LI {color: red; font-family: Verdana}
    -->
  </STYLE>
</HEAD>
<BODY>
  <P>A normal paragraph with blue text in courier.</P>
  <P>Another paragraph with blue text in courier.</P>
  <UL>
    <LI>A list in red and verdana.</LI>
  </UL>
</BODY>
</HTML>
```

In order to link a stylesheet, as in Figure 10.5, the following steps are necessary:

1 Insert the tag <LINK> between <HEAD> and </HEAD> after the title.

2 This tag contains the following elements:

- HREF indicates where the stylesheet file is. Here a relative link can be used as well as an absolute link.
- REL shows the browser what kind of linked file it is. The value stylesheet indicates this.
- TYPE indicates that it is a Cascading Stylesheet.
- TITLE assigns a name to the stylesheet. With this, you can distinguish between several stylesheets in one HTML document.

3 Within the <STYLE> tags you can define even more styles. These overwrite the definitions of the external stylesheets when they clash.

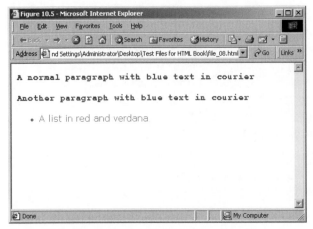

Figure 10.5: The external stylesheet shows the effect

Tip

External stylesheets are indispensable for successful Web sites. If you want to change a style, you only have to do this at a central place rather than in all documents. External stylesheets regulate the corporate design for font and links for all pages in a Web site.

Allocating a style

In this section we will show you how you can allocate styles to elements. In the last section we allocated just one style for one tag for stylesheets. We will now do more.

Note

Here we work with a stylesheet at the head of the HTML file. Of course, this would also work with external stylesheets.

One style for one tag

The allocation for a tag always follows the same pattern:

attribute   *value*   *attribute*   *value*

```
LI {color: red; font-family: Verdana}
```

First, the appropriate tag stands inside the curly brackets, then the individual style allocations, which are separated by commas. A style allocation consists of the attribute, for example `colour` or `font-family` and the value of the attribute like `red` and `verdana`. Attribute and value are separated by a colon.

If you want to provide several tags with the same style allocations, simply write the tags separated from one another with a comma. The style allocations follow each other in curly brackets.

```
P, H1 {color: blue; font-family: Arial}
```

Different styles for nested tags

Many tags, such as lists, are nested on several levels. You can allocate a style to every level, by repeating the opening tag in each one.

```
<HTML>
<HEAD>
 <TITLE>Figure 10.6</TITLE>
 <STYLE TYPE="text/css">
  <!--
  UL LI {color: red; font-family:Verdana}
  UL UL LI {color: blue; font-family:Courier}
  -->
 </STYLE>
</HEAD>
<BODY>
 <UL>
  <LI>A list in red and verdana.
  <UL>
   <LI>The subordinate list in blue and courier.</LI>
  </UL>
  </LI>
 </UL>
</BODY>
</HTML>
```

unordered list — *list item*

211

In our example the first level of the list is displayed in red and Verdana. The second is an address with `UL UL LI` and text formatted in blue and courier (see Figure 10.6).

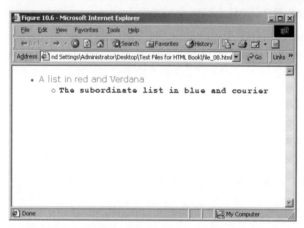

Figure 10.6: Allocating different styles to a nested list

Styles for tags in other tags

If you want to allocate just one style to a tag, and this is contained in another tag, first enter the outside tag, and then the inner tag, separated with a blank.

```
P B {color: red}
```

In the above example, all text lists in a `<B>` tag that are also contained in a `<P>` tag are displayed in red.

Styles with classes

You can determine different styles for a tag with classes. Alternatively you can create a tag-independent class which can be used for any tag. Both possibilities are shown here.

If you want to have more than one style for a tag, you have to create different classes. This can be useful for paragraphs or table cells.

You simply write the desired tag and separate the name of the class with a full stop. The style definition then follows in curly brackets.

Here is a brief example:

```
<HTML>
<HEAD>
 <TITLE>Figure 10.7</TITLE>
 <STYLE TYPE="text/css">
  <!--
  P.class1 {color: red; font-weight: bold}
  P.class2 {color: blue; font-style: italic}
  -->
 </STYLE>
</HEAD>
<BODY>
 <P CLASS="class1">A paragraph with red and bold text.</P>
 <P CLASS="class2">A paragraph with blue and italic text.</P>
 <P>A paragraph without style.</P>
</BODY>
</HTML>
```

curly bracket

In the above example the following steps are important (see also Figure 10.7):

1 A stylesheet is defined at the head of the HTML page containing two classes for the <P> tag.

2 The first class for the <P> tag is called `class1` and determines red and bold text.

3 The second class is called `class2` and with `P.` is also appropriate for the <P> tag. Here the text is blue and italic.

4 In the <P> tag you determine which class is used for a paragraph. If no class is given in the <P> tag (as in the last paragraph of our example), only one format which is indicated without a class is used.

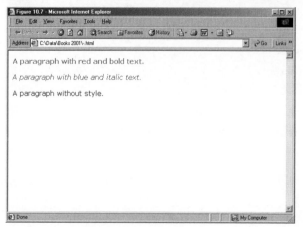

Figure 10.7: Different paragraphs are allocated various styles with classes

In order to define a class independently from a tag, write the name of the class after a full stop. However, the name of the tag before the full stop is missing, as illustrated in the following example .

```
<HTML>
<HEAD>
 <TITLE>Figure 10.8</TITLE>
 <STYLE TYPE="text/css">
  <!--
  .class1 {color: red; font-weight: bold}
  .class2 {color: blue; font-style: italic}
  -->
 </STYLE>
</HEAD>
<BODY>
 <P CLASS="class1">A paragraph with red and bold text.</P>
 <P CLASS="class2">A paragraph with blue and italic text.</
```

214

```
P>
 <UL>
  <LI CLASS="class1">
  A list with red and bold text.          .
  </LI>
 </UL>
</BODY>
</HTML>
```

To tie the general classes together, the following steps are necessary:

In the stylesheet at the head of the HTML page, define the two common classes. The full stop comes first. This indicates that it is a common class which is not assigned to a tag. The name of the class then follows with `class1` or `class2` (see Figure 10.8).

5 The style settings follow respectively in curly brackets.

6 In the tag at the head of the HTML page, the common classes are called up. The assigned text formatting only reaches the end of the respective tag.

> **Tip**
>
> *If you want to allocate one class to several tags, write the tags and seperate them from each other with commas. An example would be* `P,LI.class1`. *With this code you can inset the class with the name class1 in the* `<P>` *and* `<LI>` *tags. Of course, you can also insert a class for nested tags on various hierarchical levels. An example of this would be* `UL LI.class1`. *Thus the following styles are allocated to all list entries of the first level.*

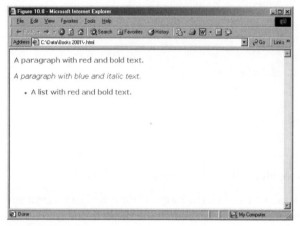

Figure 10.8: The paragraphs and the lists are formatted with common classes

Styles with IDs

In the official standard of the W3C consortium the use of IDs in place of classes is not recommended. Nevertheless we want to discuss it briefly here.

In principle, IDs work in the same way as classes (see Figure 10.9). They can be bound to tags or can be defined as common IDs. IDs are separated from the tag with a double sharp # instead of a full stop, or are indicated as common IDs. This is how they work:

```
<HTML>
<HEAD>
 <TITLE>Figure 10.9</TITLE>
 <STYLE TYPE="text/css">
  <!--
  P#ID1 {color: red; font-weight: bold}
  #ID2 {color: blue; font-style: italic}
  -->
 </STYLE>
</HEAD>
<BODY>
 <P ID="ID1">A paragraph with red and bold text.</P>
 <P ID="ID2">A paragraph with blue and italic text.</P>
 <UL>
```

```
<LI ID="ID2">
A list with blue and italic text.
</LI>
</UL>
</BODY>
</HTML>
```

In the above example the following unusual features are found:

1 You fix the IDs in the stylesheet at the head of the HTML page. The first ID is bound with P# to the <P> tag.

2 The second ID is common, since no tag stands before the double sharp #.

3 In the tag, the appropriate ID is called up with the attribute ID. The value of the attribute is the name of the respective ID. An ID that is coupled with a tag can only be used here. A common ID can be called in any tag.

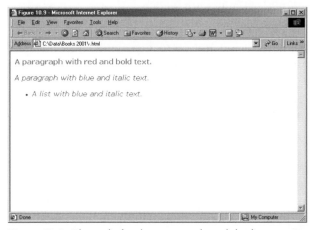

Figure 10.9: The style for the paragraph and the list are given IDs

> **Note**
> *If you insert both IDs and classes in an HTML page, the ID override the classes.*

Formatting

We will now show you some ways to format stylesheets.

Font formatting

Stylesheets offer excellent possibilities for formatting bigger text passages. We have already covered some of these techniques.

The attribute `font` contains most of the other attributes. They are simply lined up behind each other and separated by blanks.

```
P {font: italic bold 18pt Arial}
```

The sequence is important here. If it is not correct, none of the values are processed at all. The correct sequence is: `font-style`, `font-weight`, `font-size`, `font-face`.

In Table 10.1 we have summarised the most important attributes used in text formatting.

Attribute	Description	Value
`font-family`	Establishes a font family	A font (Arial) or a font family (serif, sans serif etc.)
`font-style`	Establishes a font style	italic oblique (mostly italic)
`font-variant`	Allows you to display a text in lower case only. This only works with Internet Explorer.	smallcaps
`font-size`	Establishes the size of the font	Numerical values can be given in points (pt), per-cent of the normal font size (%) or with absolute terms like small, medium and large.
`font-weight`	Strength of the text	bold numerical in a scale of 100 to 1,000 (400 = normal, 700 = bold)
`text-align`	The alignment of the text	centre justify (justification; does not work with current browsers) left right
`text-decoration`	Special text decoration	underline blink line-trough overline

Table 10.1: Attributes for formatting of fonts.

One font for the whole page

One of the areas in which font formatting is most frequently used is when a font is fixed for the whole page (see Figure 10.10). In order to do this you have to assign a font to both the <BODY> as well as the <TD> tag for the tables.

```
<HTML>
<HEAD>
 <TITLE>Figure 10.10</TITLE>
 <STYLE TYPE="text/css">
  <!--
  BODY, TD {font-family: Arial, sans-serif}
  -->
 </STYLE>
</HEAD>
<BODY>
 <H1>Heading</H1>
 <P>A normal paragraph</P>
 <TABLE>
  <TR>
   <TD>Table</TD>
  </TR>
 </TABLE>
 <UL>
  <LI>
  A list
  </LI>
 </UL>
</BODY>
</HTML>
```

The allocation of a script is carried out in the following way:

1 A stylesheet is inserted at the head of the HTML page.

2 The stylesheet contains a definition for the `<BODY>` and all `<TD>` tags (`BODY`, `TD`).

3 The style is defined in the curly brackets behind the tag. You select a font with the attribute `font-family`. In our example we have selected `Arial` and as an alternative, we have indicated another font (`sans-serif`) after the commas.

> **Note**
>
> *A sans-serif font is a font without strokes at the end of the letters. Arial and Verdana belong to this family. A font with serif (with strokes) is something like Times New Roman.*

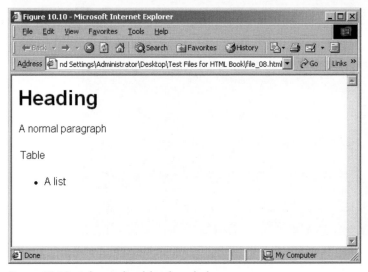

Figure 10.10: A font is fixed for the whole page

Links

There are three so-called pseudo-classes for links. There are also three conditions for a link, to which you can assign separate styles:

- `A:link` allows you to fix a style for a link that has not been visited.

- With `A:active` you can fix a style for a link that has been clicked on by the user.

- `A:visited` determines a style for a link on a page that has already been visited.

Make sure that all links that have not been activated or visited are displayed without being underlined. This function is used by many large pages. For example, Rhapsody in Bloom in Figure 10.11 (`www.rhapsody-in-bloom.com`) displays its links in red. Activated links are shown in bright red. Visited links correspond to normal links. This is achieved with a simple stylesheet:

```
A:link {color: #B20A15; text-decoration: none}

A:active {color: #FF0000; text-decoration: none}

A:visited {color: #B20A15; text-decoration: none}
```

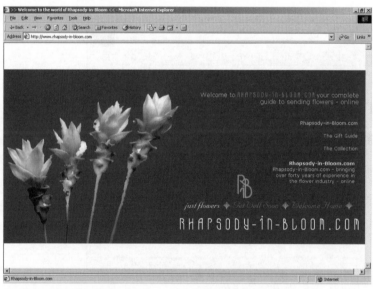

Figure 10.11: Rhapsody in Bloom displays the links in red

Paragraphs

In addition to three pseudo-classes for links there are also two more for the `<P>` tag. These are:

- `P:first-line` allows you to fix a style for the first line of a paragraph.

`P:first-letter` allows you to assign another style for the first letter of a paragraph. This function can be used to create "large" first letters in the print area.

Other examples

In this section we show you some more uses for stylesheets.

Background

You already know the attribute BACKGROUND for the <BODY> tag. In addition to this you can also fix a background for the HTML page with stylesheets.

The attribute BACKGROUND contains most of the other attributes separated by blanks. However the sequence is of no meaning here.

```
BODY {background: rgb(255, 0, 0) url(images/image.jpg)
fixed}
```

The background colour is fixed as red, and the background image as IMAGE.JPG. The background image is fixed and does not scroll. Table 10.2 describes various background attributes.

> **Note**
>
> The RGB notation of colours can be carried out with either absolute colour values or with percentage values of the RGB colours (RGB stands for Red, Green, Blue.

Attribute	Description	Value
background-attachment	Determines whether or not the background image can be scrolled	fixed scroll (default setting)
background-color	Background colour	Colours in hexadecimal notation, as colour name or with the RGB colour value. transparent (transparent background)
background-image	Address of the background image	url(Address) (For the address you indicate a relative of an absolute link) transparent (no background image, standard setting)
background-position	The position of the background image in the x/y coordinate system. Zero is at the top left corner of the window.	Coordinates in pixels or percentages (e.g. background-position: 100 100). top centre bottom left right
background-repeat	Determines how the background image is repeated	repeat (horizontally and vertically repeated; default setting) repeat-x (horizontally repeated) repeat-y (vertically repeated) no-repeat (background image is not repeated)

Table 10.2: Attributes for background.

Distances

In addition to normal attributes for the background you can also adjust the distances of all objects from the edge of the window. The attribute `margin` for the `<BODY>` tag is used for this purpose.

```
BODY {margin: 60px 40px}
```

The left value indicates the distance above and below, and the right value indicates the distance left and right (see Figure 10.12).

> Note
>
> *Possible values are given in pixels (px), percentages (%) or inches (in). If you switch to auto, the distance is determined by the browser.*

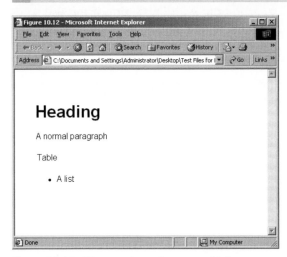

Figure 10.12: Distance from the top and left

Further attributes control the distance in all four directions, one by one (see Table 10.3):

Attribute	Description	Values
margin-bottom	Distance from the bottom	Linear measurement or percentage value
margin-left	Distance from the left	Linear measurement or percentage value
margin-right	Distance from the right	Linear measurement or percentage value
margin-top	Distance from the top	Linear measurement or percentage value

Table 10.3: Attributes for distance from the edge of the window.

Rollover effect

Normally the rollover effect is carried out with JavaScript. If the user runs over an image provided through a link with a mouse, it changes colour (see Figure 10.13). This was not possible for text links until now; therefore all texts which should be provided with a rollover effect are saved as images.

The pseudo-class A:hover eliminates this problem, but only for Internet Explorer and Opera. Netscape does not support this function.

Tip

Since in most cases no functional disadvantages arise from lack of a rollover effect for the Netscape user, you can use it without worrying.

Here is how this works:

```
<HTML>
<HEAD>
 <TITLE>Figure 10.13</TITLE>
 <STYLE TYPE="text/css">
  <!--
  A:hover {color: yellow}
  A:link {color: red}
  A:active {color: red}
```

```
    A:visited {color: blue}
    -->
  </STYLE>
</HEAD>
<BODY>
 <A HREF="#">A link</H>
</BODY>
</HTML>
```

Here, you should note the following:

1 The pseudo-class A:hover is defined in the stylesheet at the head of the HTML page.

2 Here you provide a different format from that of a normal link (A:link). In our example we have changed the colour of the text to yellow (color: yellow).

3 The other pseudo-classes should also be defined, otherwise the default settings of the browser are used.

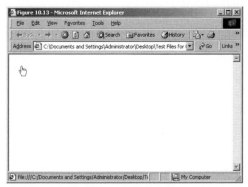

Figure 10.13: The colour of the link changes when run over with the mouse

Frames

Stylesheets can also be used to set frames for an object. The object can be a paragraph, a heading, an image, or a table (see Figure 10.14).

With border you carry this out in the same way using the attributes: frame colour, frame width, frame style. The sequence is not important. You can only define border for tables if you combine it with the <TABLE> tag. In this example we define the frames as a common class.

```
<HTML>
<HEAD>
 <TITLE>Figure 10.14</TITLE>
 <STYLE TYPE="text/css">
  <!--
   .frame1 {border: double 15px red}
  -->
 </STYLE>
</HEAD>
<BODY>
 <P CLASS="frame1">paragraph with frame</P>
</BODY>
</HTML>
```

The following steps are necessary:

1 First determine a common class with the name `frame1`.

2 In the curly brackets you will find the attribute `border`. This contains information about the frame.

3 The first bit of information is about the style of the frame, such as `double`.

4 Next, the width of the frame is set at `15px`.

5 Last is the colour of the frame. This can be given in either hexadecimal notation, with the colour name, or as a RGB value. In this example we have chosen red (`red`).

6 In the appropriate tag to which you want to apply the frame, simply call up the class (`CLASS="frame1"`). See Figure 10.14.

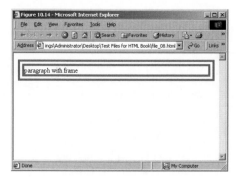

Figure 10.14: A frame for a paragraph

In addition to `border` there are also many other attributes for frames (see Figure 10.15). Many of these are already contained in `border`. We list the most important ones in Table 10.4:

Attribute	Description	Values
`border-color`	Colour of the border	As a hexadecimal value, with the colour name or as a RGB value (absolute and percentage)
`border-style`	Style of the frame. Be careful as most effects only work in Internet Explorer. Normally one should avoid effects since they are displayed in a non-uniform way.	`none` (no frames are shown) `double` (double) `groove` (frames with simulated lighting; see Figure 10.15) `inset` (3D-effect with colour effect inside) `outset` (3D-effect with colour effect outside) `ridge` (3D-effect) `solid` (normally in monochrome) Apart from this there are two values: `dashed` and `dotted`. These are not displayed by either of the two current browsers.
`border-width`	Width of the frame	Linear measurements such as pixels (px), centimetres (cm) or inches (in) `medium` `thin` `thick`

Table 10.4: Further attributes for frames

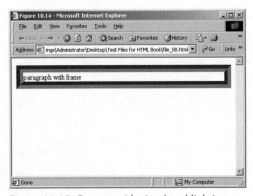

Figure 10.15: Frames with simulated lighting

Placing elements

Exact placment of elements is vital in good Web design. The classic method uses invisible tables and 1-pixel-GIFs. An alternative is using layers. The <LAYER> tag was introduced in Netscape 4, but has never been implemented in Internet Explorer.

With CSS you can control the position of objects. This is carried out using the two tags <DIV> and <SPAN>. Great effects can be achieved with a bit of JavaScript.

Therefore positioning with Cascading Stylesheets works in most cases with the tags <DIV> and </DIV>. To explain:

```
<HTML>

<HEAD>
```

```
<TITLE>Figure 10.16</TITLE>
</HEAD>
<BODY>
<DIV STYLE="position:absolute; top:100px; left:100px;
➥width:200px"><P>A positioned paragraph</P></DIV>
</BODY>
</HTML>
```

You determine the different attributes for positioning in the STYLE attribute. For this example, the following steps are necessary:

1 Put the <DIV>– and the </DIV> tag around the paragraph.

2 Add the attribute STYLE to the <DIV> tag.

3 The attribute STYLE contains several attributes which indicate the position of the element in the <DIV> tag.

4 The attribute position indicates the kind of positioning. There are the following options:

- absolute always fixes an element absolutely the same distance from the edge of the window.

- fixed places an element at a fixed distance, though the element is not scrolled if you move the scroll bar. Unfortunately this option is not supported by any current browsers.

- relative always orientates the position of the element to its predeccesor. If this is bigger than is allowed by the position of the successor, it directly follows the predecessor.

- static retains the normal order of the individual elements. This is the default setting.

5 In principle, the distance instructions also start from the top and the left. You can do this with the attributes top and left as well as a linear measurement.

> **Note**
>
> *As well as distance from the top and the left you can also determine distance from the bottom and the right with* bottom *and* right.

6 The attribute width indicates the width of the element. A linear measurement is also inserted here.

Chapter 11

Frames

*We are now going to show you how to use frames,
what you must pay attention to, and what the
advantages and disadvantages of using frames are.*

Take a look at Figure 11.1. The browser window is divided into three. On the left and at the top there are areas for navigation, and on the right, an area for the contents. Each of these has its own scrollbar, so they can all be scrolled independently of each other. These areas are called frames.

Figure 11.1: Three frames in a Web page

Defining framesets

Before we go any further, we need to make some basic preparations:

1 Create `file1.html` according to the following pattern:

```
<HTML>
<HEAD>
<TITLE>1. Frame</TITLE>
</HEAD>
<BODY BGCOLOR="white">
<H3>1. Frame</H3>
</BODY>
</HTML>
```

2 Create the files `2.html`, `3.html`, `4.html` and `5.html` in the same way.

New tags

In order to work with frames we have to introduce two new tags:

- `<FRAMESET>` – defines the division of an area into individual frames
- `<FRAME>` – indicates a single frame

An HTML page then has the following general construction:

```
<HTML>
<HEAD>
   <TITLE>Frames</TITLE>
</HEAD>
<FRAMESET>
   <!-- several Frames -->
</FRAMESET>
<BODY BGCOLOR="white">
However, at this stage, your browser cannot display any
frames.
</BODY>
</HTML>
```

Dividing areas

You can divide up an area, at the start using the browser window, horizontally or vertically. Which ever you choose, indicate it as an attribute in the `<FRAMESET>` tag:

- `COLS="..."` divides the area vertically into *columns*
- `ROWS="..."` divides the area horizontally into *rows*

Give the size of a single frame as the value of the attribute in `COLS` or `ROWS`, separated from each other by commas. You can also use percentages, for example:

```
<FRAMESET COLS="50%,50%">
   <!-- several frames -->
</FRAMESET>
```

Thus the area is divided vertically into two columns.

```
<FRAMESET ROWS="33%,33%,34%">
   <!-- several frames -->
</FRAMESET>
```

The above listing divides the area horizontally into three rows as in Figure 11.2.

The question now is, which files land up in which frame. The <FRAME> tag is responsible for this and is allocated to each frame. In the SRC attribute the file name of the HTML page which is to be loaded in the frame is given. It behaves like the links in Chapter 4: so you can use relative or absolute paths.

Now you can see why you had to create the five files earlier- these are used as a visualisation of the frame sets. Next is a frame set with two columns which both take 50% of the width of the area:

```
<HTML>
<HEAD>
   <TITLE>Frames</TITLE>
</HEAD>
<FRAMESET COLS="50%,50%">
   <FRAME SRC="1.html">
   <FRAME SRC="2.html">
</FRAMESET>
<BODY BGCOLOR="white">
Again your browser cannot display any frames!
</BODY>
</HTML>
```

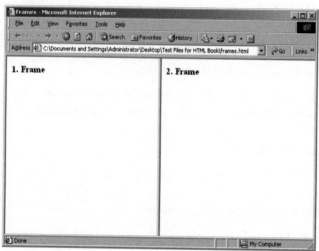

Figure 11.2: Two vertical frames

The following listing divides the area into three rows which are all of the same height (see Figure 11.3):

```
<HTML>
<HEAD>
   <TITLE>Frames</TITLE>
</HEAD>
<FRAMESET ROWS="33%,33%,34%">
   <FRAME SRC="1.html">
   <FRAME SRC="2.html">
   <FRAME SRC="3.html">
</FRAMESET>
<BODY BGCOLOR="white">
Your browser cannot display any frames.
</BODY>
</HTML>
```

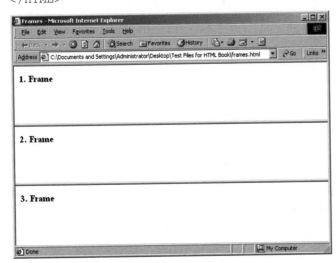

Figure 11.3: Three horizontal frames

At this point you may ask how we actually define another <BODY> area. Not all browsers understand frames, for example the browsers on many hand held computers. For these the alternative text is then shown. In the section "Why frames?" we show you what this can look like.

In the following listings we leave out the basic frameborder of HTML and only show the frame set.

Fixed height and width

Using percentages, you can also give heights (or widths) in pixels. Take a look at the following frameset (see Figure 11.4):

```
<FRAMESET COLS="250,350">
  <FRAME SRC="1.html">
  <FRAME SRC="2.html">
</FRAMESET>
```

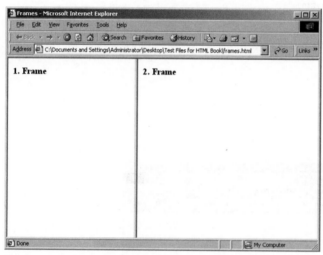

Figure 11.4: 250 pixels wide on the left, on the right, 350 pixels

In Figure 11.4 the browser area is divided into two vertical frames, the left frame is 250 pixels wide, and the right is 350 pixels wide. You can see that the area shown is exactly 600 pixels wide. But what happens if another screen size is selected? For example if the user's screen has a different height or a particularly low resolution. Try this out by changing the width of the browser window. You can see the results in Figures 11.5 and 11.6.

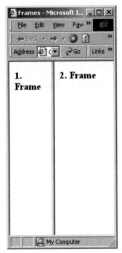

Figure 11.5: The browser window is smaller

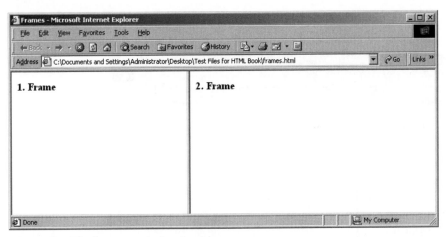

Figure 11.6: The browser window is wider

You can see that to some extent the browser has tried to maintain the proportions of the two frame widths (here 5:7). You cannot rely on the fact that all browsers do this (although Netscape Navigator and Internet Explorer do), because these proportions are not prescribed. In addition, sometimes a browser leaves the left hand frame fixed, and adapts the right hand frame correspondingly. Therefore, if you want to have proportional widths, you must insert percentage values.

Remaining height and width

The example illustrated in Figure 11.7 frequently occurs in practice. You have a navigation bar on the left, and a contents bar on the right. The navigation bar has a fixed width of about 150 pixels, because you know exactly which navigation points and/or graphics will stand there. The remaining browser area is reserved for the contents. The formulation is clear: the left frame will be exactly 150 pixels wide , the rest will be assigned to the right frame. Up until now this has not been possible.

The solution lies with the star symbol (*). You can insert the star as a width or height instruction, with the meaning "as much as is left". Therefore the following frameset definition divides the area into two vertical frames; the left is exactly 150 pixels wide, and the right takes up the remaining space, but is independent from the browser size, as follows:

```
<FRAMESET COLS="150,*">
  <FRAME SRC="1.html">
  <FRAME SRC="2.html">
</FRAMESET>
```

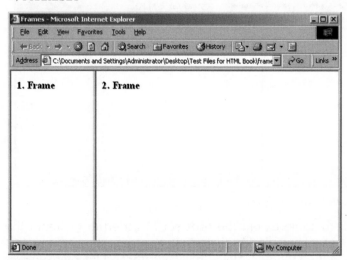

Figure 11.7: The left frame is always exactly 150 pixels wide, while the right can alter to fit the space

You can also mix the different units of measurement with each other. Divide up the browser window into three frames: the middle frame will be half as wide as the whole window, the right frame will be exactly 111 pixels. The following HTML code converts this as follows (Figure 11.8):

```
<FRAMESET COLS="*,50%,111">
  <FRAME SRC="1.html">
  <FRAME SRC="2.html">
  <FRAME SRC="3.html">
</FRAMESET>
```

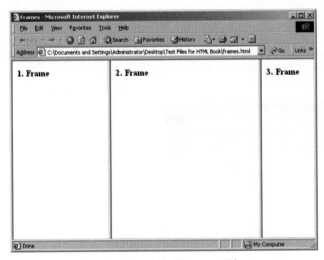

Figure 11.8: Three frames with different widths

Proportional height and width

Newer browsers have another way of dividing. Assume that you have the formulation to divide the browser area vertically into two frames and that the widths will be at a ratio of 5:7 to each other.

The browser tries to keep the proportional representation, scaling the frames correspondingly. If you want to proceed accurately, however, use the star operator:

```
<FRAMESET COLS="5*,7*">
  <FRAME SRC="1.html">
  <FRAME SRC="2.html">
</FRAMESET>
```

Parts of the area above are divided vertically into two frames, where the first and the second frames have a ratio of 5:7.

You can also use percentage values, but these are rounded up and therefore less precise.

You can also mix these kinds of measurements, though not with the star itself, as follows:

```
<FRAMESET COLS="2*,50%,3*">
    <FRAME SRC="1.html">
    <FRAME SRC="2.html">
    <FRAME SRC="3.html">
</FRAMESET>
```

which shows three frames: The middle one is half as wide as the browser window and the right frame is one and a half times as wide as the left frame. You can see the result in Figure 11.9

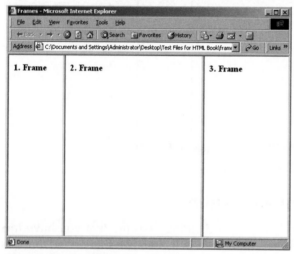

Figure 11.9: The ratio of the left to the right frame is 2:3

Nesting frames

Until now it has been quite simple and easy to understand. Using the attribute in the <FRAMESET> tag you can see how many frames are contained in the frameset, and the appropriate number of <FRAME> tags you have to use. Leaf back through the book and look at Figure 11.1 again. The division shown there is still not possible with our current means... or is it?

To simplify the problem we must divide the browser area into three frames: two at the top, and one at the bottom.

It is clear that the area has to be divided twice, both horizontally and vertically. And here is the trick.

1 First divide the area horizontally:

```
<FRAMESET ROWS="67%,*">
  <FRAME SRC="frame1.html">
  <FRAME SRC="3.html">
</FRAMESET>
```

2 Second load the page in your browser. It should look roughly like Figure 11.10.

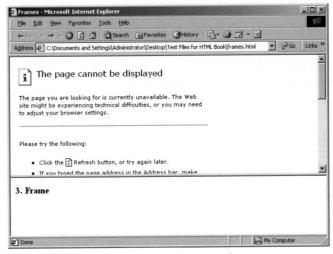

Figure 11.10: First divide the area horizontally

In the bottom frame the file `frame3.html` is loaded. In the top frame, an error message appears as the file `frame1.html` does not yet exist. In this file the area can be divided vertically so we have accomplished our task. Create a file `frame1.html` according to the following pattern:

```
<HTML>
<HEAD>
  <TITLE>Frames</TITLE>
</HEAD>
<FRAMESET COLS="150,*">
  <FRAME SRC="1.html">
  <FRAME SRC="2.html">
</FRAMESET>
</HTML>
```

243

You have now divided the browser page into three, as you can see in Figure 11.11.

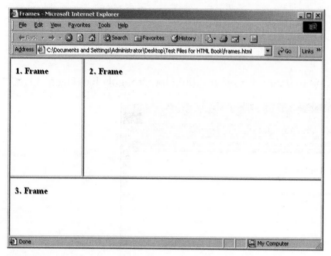

Figure 11.11: The browser area is divided into three

You can, however, save yourself from detouring to an external file. Take another look at the original frameset:

```
<FRAMESET ROWS="67%,*">
  <FRAME SRC="frame1.html">
  <FRAME SRC="3.html">
</FRAMESET>
```

Define two frames and use a `<FRAME>` tag for each. By using these `<FRAME>` tags you can also use another frameset:

```
<FRAMESET ROWS="67%,*">
  <!-- 1. "Frame" -->
  <FRAMESET COLS="150,*">
    <FRAME SRC="1.html">
    <FRAME SRC="2.html">
  </FRAMESET>
  <!-- 2. Frame -->
  <FRAME SRC="3.html">
</FRAMESET>
```

Of course, this example can be more complicated. The following code creates five frames (see Figure 11.12). Though one has to ask, whether this is acceptable with low resolution:

```
<FRAMESET ROWS="67%,*">
  <FRAMESET COLS="2*,3*,2*">
    <FRAME SRC="1.html">
    <FRAMESET ROWS="2*,1*">
      <FRAME SRC="2.html">
      <FRAME SRC="3.html">
    </FRAMESET>
    <FRAME SRC="4.html">
  </FRAMESET>
  <FRAME SRC="5.html">
</FRAMESET>
```

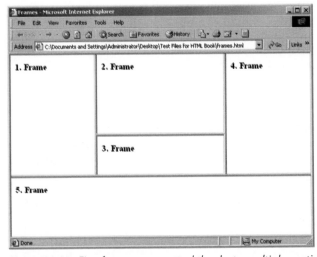

Figure 11.12: Five frames are created thanks to multiple nesting

Formatting framesets

This is as far as we want to go in individual frames. We now come to formatting.

Changing frame sizes

Using the mouse, click once on the thick grey bars between the single frames. You can now change the size of the frames. For you, the user, this is not a bad thing, as you can adapt the screen division as you wish (within certain limits). From the screen designer's point of view, though, the whole thing is a nightmare, because when the size of the frames is changed, a carefully polished layout is ruined. For this reason, in practice you cannot change the size of a frame.

In order to resolve this, you have to insert NORESIZE into at least one of the frames involved. Here is the example from Figure 11.12, this time supplemented with NORESIZE:

```
<FRAMESET ROWS="67%,*">
   <FRAMESET COLS="2*,3*,2*">
     <FRAME SRC="1.html">
     <FRAMESET ROWS="2*,1*">
       <FRAME SRC="2.html" NORESIZE>
       <FRAME SRC="3.html">
     </FRAMESET>
     <FRAME SRC="4.html">
   </FRAMESET>
   <FRAME SRC="5.html">
</FRAMESET>
```

Take another look at Figure 11.12. The size of frame 2 cannot be changed any more. It is also clear that frames 1 and 4 cannot be made either smaller or wider, as this would change the width of frame 2. Therefore pay attention to side effects using NORESIZE.

Frame 5 can, however, be made as tall or short as you like, as only frames 1, 3 and 4 are influenced by this.

But what happens now, if the size of frame 3 cannot be changed any more?

```
<FRAMESET ROWS="67%,*">
   <FRAMESET COLS="2*,3*,2*">
```

```
  <FRAME SRC="1.html">
  <FRAMESET ROWS="2*,1*">
    <FRAME SRC="2.html">
    <FRAME SRC="3.html" NORESIZE>
  </FRAMESET>
  <FRAME SRC="4.html">
 </FRAMESET>
 <FRAME SRC="5.html">
</FRAMESET>
```

Take a look at 11.12. Frame 3 is adjoined to all other frames, therefore no other frames can be changed in size.

If you want to set it so that no frame can be changed in size, you have to laboriously work out which frame you need to equip with NORESIZE. In the end it is easier to use NORESIZE in all <FRAME> tags.

Scrollbars

Automatic scrolling is a wonderful thing. It means that the whole contents of a window or a frame is visible on low resolution screens as well. In Figure 11.1 you saw this particularly clearly, because every window had a scrollbar. However, there are cases in which a scrollbar is not wanted. For example, if a frame only contains a graphic that is bigger than the frame. You can set whether a frame contains scrollbars or not by attaching the attribute SCROLLING of the <FRAME> tags to one of these three values:

- auto – Default value. Automatically determines whether scrollbars are shown or not on the basis of the content of the frame.

- yes – Scrollbars are shown in every case.

- no – Scrollbars are not shown in any case.

The input of SCROLLING="yes" is unnecessary for the most part, as you can see in the following example:

```
<FRAMESET ROWS="67%,*">
  <FRAMESET COLS="2*,3*,2*">
    <FRAME SRC="1.html" SCROLLING="yes">
    <FRAMESET ROWS="2*,1*">
      <FRAME SRC="2.html" SCROLLING="yes">
      <FRAME SRC="3.html" SCROLLING="yes">
```

```
</FRAMESET>

  <FRAME SRC="4.html" SCROLLING="yes">

</FRAMESET>

  <FRAME SRC="5.html" SCROLLING="yes">

</FRAMESET>
```

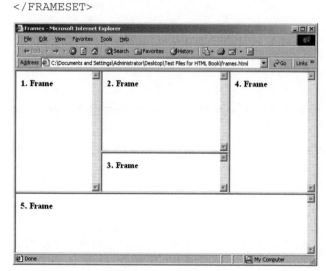

Figure 11.13: Every frame has a scrollbar

As you can see in Figure 11.13, every frame now has a scrollbar. Figure 11.14 shows the result of SCROLLING="no":

```
<FRAMESET COLS="50,*">

  <FRAME SRC="1.html" SCROLLING="no">

  <FRAME SRC="2.html">

</FRAMESET>
```

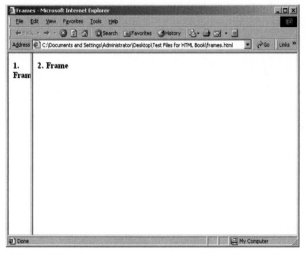

Figure 11.14: The left frame has no scrollbars

The left frame has no scroll bars, which is why the text is not displayed fully.

Frame borders

The examples up until now have not been particularly aesthetically pleasing. The thick grey bar between frames is – particularly in polished layouts – unattractive. To improve the look you can put a frameborder around a frame.

Internet Explorer and Netscape Navigator behave very differently when dealing with frameborders. The following attributes are available in the `<FRAMESET>` tag:

- `BORDER` – indicates the width of the frameborder in pixels. This is only supported by Netscape Navigator.

- `FRAMEBORDER` – indicates whether a frameborder is to be shown (`"yes"`) or not (`"no"`). This is only supported by Internet Explorer.

- `FRAMESPACING` – indicates the width of the frameborder in pixels. This is again only supported by Internet Explorer.

If you want to completely avoid frame borders, you have to use a combination of the three attributes (see Figure 11.15):

```
<FRAMESET
    BORDER="0" FRAMEBORDER="0" FRAMESPACING="0">
```

Applied to the example with the five frames you get:

```
<FRAMESET ROWS="67%,*"
  BORDER="0" FRAMEBORDER="0" FRAMESPACING="0">
  <FRAMESET COLS="2*,3*,2*"
    BORDER="0" FRAMEBORDER="0" FRAMESPACING="0">
    <FRAME SRC="1.html">
    <FRAMESET ROWS="2*,1*"
      BORDER="0" FRAMEBORDER="0" FRAMESPACING="0">
      <FRAME SRC="2.html">
      <FRAME SRC="3.html">
    </FRAMESET>
    <FRAME SRC="4.html">
  </FRAMESET>
  <FRAME SRC="5.html">
</FRAMESET>
```

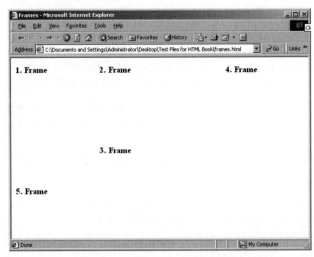

Figure 11.15: The frames are now without frameborders

Without frameborders the individual frames cannot be distinguished from each other by their contents or by scrollbars.

If you really want to use frameborders (or have to) you can indicate the thickness as the value for the corresponding attribute. In the attribute BORDERCOLOR of the <FRAMESET> tag you can set the colour:

```
<FRAMESET ROWS="67%,*" BORDERCOLOR="black">
  <FRAMESET COLS="2*,3*,2*" BORDERCOLOR="yellow">
    <FRAME SRC="1.html">
    <FRAMESET ROWS="2*,1*" BORDERCOLOR="red">
      <FRAME SRC="2.html">
      <FRAME SRC="3.html">
    </FRAMESET>
    <FRAME SRC="4.html">
  </FRAMESET>
  <FRAME SRC="5.html">
</FRAMESET>
```

Links

Here we will create another HTML file named links.html using the following:

```
<HTML>
<HEAD>
  <TITLE>Links</TITLE>
</HEAD>
<BODY BGCOLOR="white">
<A HREF="5.html">Link</A>
</BODY>
</HTML>
```

We will now modify this file further, but only using one row in the link.

The frameset is as follows:

```
<FRAMESET COLS="150,*">
  <FRAME SRC="links.html">
  <FRAME SRC="1.html">
</FRAMESET>
```

Click on the link and see what happens (or take a look at Figure 11.16).

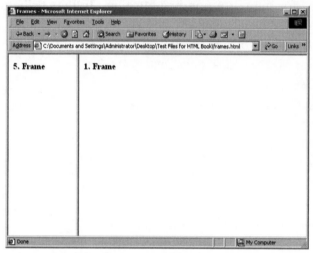

Figure 11.16: The link opens itself in the left hand frame

It is often the case that navigation is in the left hand frame, and contents in the right. The link will therefore be opened in the right hand frame. In order to manage this, you first have to adapt the frameset slightly (in the following we go into the file called *frames.html*):

```
<FRAMESET COLS="150,*">

  <FRAME SRC="links.html" NAME="Navigation">

  <FRAME SRC="1.html" NAME="Content">

</FRAMESET>
```

Make sure that only two frames have a NAME attribute. As discussed in Chapter 4 you can open links in a new or another window by using the attribute TARGET. If you have used a character string as a TARGET attribute, you open all links in a new window if you always use the same character string. This is the same with frames. If you give the NAME attribute of the destination frame as the TARGET attribute, the link will open there and not in the current frame. Therefore, adapt the file *links.html* in the following way:

```
<A HREF="5.html" TARGET="Content">Link</A>
```

Now the link opens in the right hand frame (see Figure 11.17).

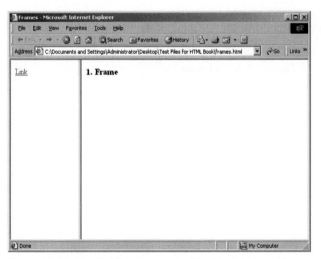

Figure 11.17: The link is now opened in the right hand frame

As well as the name of the frame, the following identifiers are available to you as TARGET attributes:

- _blank – opened in a new window.
- _parent – opened in the primary frameset.
- _self – opened in the current frame (default).
- _top – opened in the same window.

As with links, you can also set a default TARGET attribute with <BASE TARGET="...">. However in the case of individual links, these entries overwrite those of the TARGET attribute.

To play around with links a little, amend the file *links.html* again:

```
<A HREF="frames.html" TARGET="Content">Link</A><BR>
<A HREF="frames.html" TARGET="_parent">_parent</A>
<BR><A HREF="frames.html" TARGET="_self">_self</A>
<BR><A HREF="frames.html" TARGET="_top">_top</A>
```

So that the results are more visible, you should also amend the frameset:

```
<FRAMESET COLS="50%,50%">
  <FRAME SRC="links.html" NAME="Navigation">
  <FRAME SRC="1.html" NAME="Content">
</FRAMESET>
```

Now load the new frameset in the browser and click on the uppermost link. In the right hand frame (NAME attribute Content) the frameset is opened once more (see Figure 11.18).

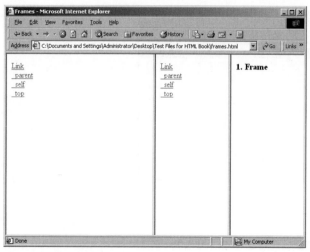

Figure 11.18: The frameset was opened once again in the right hand frame

Now look at the middle frame. You have four possible choices:

- If you click on the first link, the browser has to choose which frame to open the frameset in as there are now two frames with the NAME attribute Content. All browsers choose the frame which is nearer the top, in this case the right of the browser window. Therefore the appearance does not change.

- If you click on the second link the higher frame is opened. The higher frame is the right of the browser window, the frame with former NAME attribute Content. This is also unchanged.

- If you click on the third link, the frameset in the middle frame is opened once again. You then have four frames with a width ratio of 4:1:1:2 (see Figure 11.19).

- If you click on the fourth link, the frameset in the whole browser window is opened (and the frame structure is ruined). You get two frames, both with the same width.

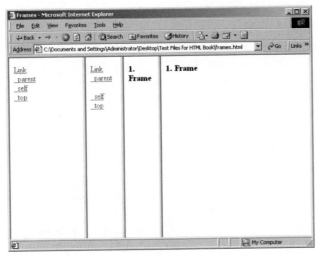

Figure 11.19: The frames have the ratio 4:1:1:2

Why frames?

Just a few notes to finish with: Frames are a good thing as they save on typing if, for example, you place navigation points into the frame. The navigation points must then be placed on one HTML page and not on all of them. If you change a navigation point, you therefore only have to change *one* file, and not all of them.

On the other hand, frames have their disadvantages. They take up space, and in view of the growing use of hand-held computers and terminals with small displays, this is a problem. Some hand-held browsers cannot cope with frames. Therefore you should at least offer the most important links in the <BODY> section of the frame page.

In this context the <NOFRAMES> tag is useful. Everything that stands between <NOFRAMES> and </NOFRAMES> is ignored by browsers that can interpret frames. Therefore, you can acommodate the following code in the <BODY> section of all contents pages:

```
<NOFRAMES>

<P>

   <A HREF="/product/">Product</A> |

   <A HREF="/press/">Press</A> |

   <A HREF="/contact/">Contact</A>

</P>

</NOFRAMES>
```

These navigation links would then be shown on PDAs (and are also important for navigation). Modern browsers ignore the whole and do not show navigation points. They do not have to do this at all as these are (hopefully) in the navigation frame!

You should also test your frame structure with the lowest possible resolution. Nothing is more painful than if important navigation points are no longer visible in a frame with low resolution (lots of people still use a resolution of 800x600 on their screen, many even as low as 640x480). The Web site cannot be navigated at this level.

> **Note**
>
> *Within a frame you can easily link to different servers. In the address field of the browser, the URL will always be shown, even if completely different things are shown in the contents frame. This is not only offensive, but possibly illegal - there have already been prosecutions because of this. Therefore the rule of thumb is: external links should always be opened in a new window.*

Chapter 12

Branching out

We will now show you how to assign information to search engines and other services in an HTML page. You will then learn how to put pages onto a server. Finally, we look at registration of Web sites with different types of search engines.

Meta tags

Meta tags are found at the head of a HTML page. Here, information is contained about the originator and contents of the page.

The tag `<META>` has to be placed between `<HEAD>` and `</HEAD>`.

Within it various pieces of information with several attributes are defined. For example, the following code line indicates the name of the author of the HTML page:

```
<META NAME="AUTHOR" CONTENT="Christian Wenz">
```

The attribute `NAME` determines what kind of information is contained in the `<META>` tag. For example, `AUTHOR` or `DESCRIPTION`, which stands for a description of the contents of the HTML page. For every Meta tag there is a `CONTENT` attribute. The relevant information is typed in here.

If you want to give several pieces of information for a page, simply insert several `<META>` tags one after another, as follows.

```
<HEAD>
 <TITLE>Figure 12.1</TITLE>
  <META NAME="AUTHOR" CONTENT="Christian Wenz">
  <META NAME="DESCRIPTION" CONTENT="Description of the
page">
</HEAD>
```

Different kinds of information

Here we introduce the most important kinds of information which can be surrounded by `<META>` tags:

- `AUTHOR` This refers to the author of the Web site.

- `PUBLISHER` works in the same way as `AUTHOR`. In most case this is not needed. Therefore, simply leave it out.

- `DESCRIPTION` allows you to input a descriptive text for the page. This text is displayed on the results page of many search engines.

- `KEYWORDS` allow you to indicate the key words which characterise the content of the page. In the attribute `CONTENT` the keywords are separated with commas. Search engines use these keywords, among other things, to assign single search strings to pages.

```
<META NAME="KEYWORDS" CONTENT="HTML, Tag, Attribute">
```

Note

Keywords are very important for search engines, but are not the only criterion. Sometimes the title of a page or the domain name is more important.

Caution

Do not try to select terms that have nothing to do with the page. This can be legally dubious with household names such as Claudia Schiffer, Britney Spears, Mercedes. It does not help if the keywords are repeated often or are written several times in the HTML page, as most search engines filter this out. At best it ignores them, at worst, you will be removed from the search engine.

- COPYRIGHT assigns a copyright note.

```
<META NAME="COPYRIGHT" CONTENT="&copy; 2001 by Tobias
➥Hauser">
```

Tip

In HTML the copyright character is represented by the special character ©.

- DATE indicates how up-to-date the page is. This can also indicate when the page needs to updated. Since you will probably not know when you intend to update your pages, you should leave this out.

```
<META NAME="DATE" CONTENT="2001-02-01">
```

The date, separated by hyphens, is given in the American format (month before day) so that English language search engines can cope with it.

- ROBOTS instructs the robots of a search engine to index the page in a certain way.

```
<META NAME="ROBOTS" CONTENT="INDEX,FOLLOW">
```

In our example we have set the value of ROBOTS to INDEX, FOLLOW. This tells the robot that it is to index the page and follow all links to the page.

Index is the default setting from which most search engines run. FOLLOW instructs the robot to, literally, follow all the links to the page. With NOFOLLOW the search machine is forbidden to do this.

NOINDEX (or NONE) tells the robot that it should not put the page in the index. Additionally you can also select the value FOLLOW or NOFOLLOW in NOINDEX.

Other functions of meta tags

Until now we have only learnt the basic function of the <META> tag. However, there are more functions for which the attribute HTTP-EQUIV is used. Instructions which the Web browser views as part of the normal header of the HTTP protocol are hidden here.

Here we want to give you an area of use for the attribute TTP-EQUIV .

```
<META HTTP-EQUIV="REFRESH" CONTENT="10;
```

➥URL=http://www.pearsoned.com">

With the value REFRESH the browser is instructed to open a new page. First, indicate after how many seconds this should happen under CONTENT. You should then give the address of the new page, separated by commas. In our example this is the Pearson Education homepage.

> **Tip**
>
> *If you require automatic forwarding, simply switch the value of the new load under* CONTENT *to 0.*

Putting your pages online

If you have finished your pages, you can now put them onto the Internet. In order to do so, you need space on a Web server. This is a computer which is constantly connected to the Internet. In most cases you will not have your very own Web server, but will be renting a so-called host space. However If you work in a company, it may have its own Web server with a constant connection to the Internet.

You can acquire the access data for your space on the server from the appropriate authority (the host or the server administrator in the company). You load the data in this space with a FTP program. FTP stands for File Transfer Protocol. This is an Internet protocol which is used for the transfer of data.

Transferring data to the server using FTP

There are various FTP programs. In this section we will use WS_FTP LE.

> **Note**
>
> *WS_FTP LE is the Light-Version of WS_FTP. It is one of the most well known FTP programs. However, it is only licensed for private use. An alternative is, for example, LeechFTP.*

To transfer the data to the server proceed in the following way:

1 First download and install WS_FTP LE. You can find this under
www.wsftp.com/cgi/download_eval.pl?product=main. You have to fill in a form and then select WS_FTP LE from the list (see Figure 12.1).

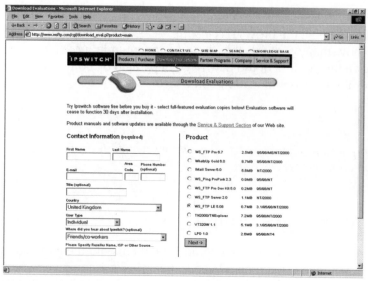

Figure 12.1: Downloading WS_FTP from the Internet

2 After you have downloaded and installed WS_FTP, start it up (see Figure 12.2).

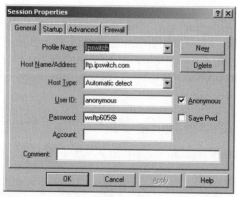

Figure 12.2: The starting screen of WS FTP

3 You can now create a profile. Click on NEW (see Figure 12.3).

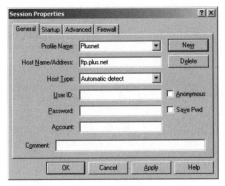

Figure 12.3: A new profile is created

4 The previous settings of the profile are now cleared. You now have to give the following details:

- With PROFILE NAME you provide a name for the profile. In our example this is PLUSNET.

- The HOST NAME is given by your host or server administrator. For the most part this is an address in the form `domain.net` or `ftp.domain.net`.

- You leave out HOST TYPE unless you alrady know which server you are using.

- USER ID and PASSWORD are also given by your host or server administrator.

> **Note**
>
> *The check box ANONYMOUS logs you onto a server without a User ID and Password. This only works with commonly accessible servers which are offered by FTP Downloads.*

- With the option SAVE PWD you can save the password, so you don't have to remember it (however, anyone who has access to the computer also has access to the FTP-Server).

5 In STARTUP you can select another default folder in the INITIAL local folder, with which WS FTP is started up (see Figure 12.4). This should be the folder in which the finished version of your Web site is placed.

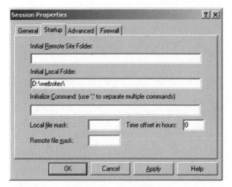

Figure 12.4: Choose a local folder in STARTUP

6 Now, in order to register on the server, make sure you are connected to the Internet and press OK.

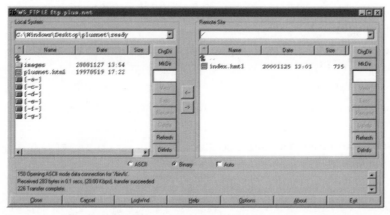

Figure 12.5: The local folder is on the left hand side and the server, on the right

In order to upload data, highlight it and select the arrow pointing right in the middle of the page between the local folder and the server (see Figures 12.5 and 12.6).

> **Note**
>
> *In the context menu of a file you can also use the command TRANSFER FILE in order to upload the file. In addition you can highlight several files and upload fthem by depressing the ⬆ or Ctrl key.*

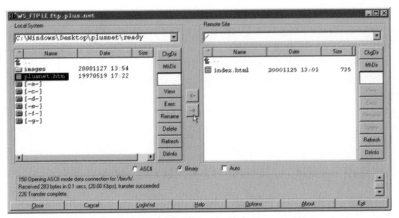

Figure 12.6: Click on the arrow pointing right to upload the file

7 Now the file is on the server (see Figure 12.7). The download works in the opposite direction i.e. you highlight files on the server and click on the arrow pointing left towards the local folder.

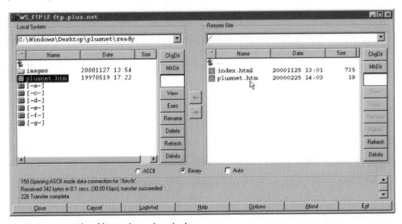

Figure 12.7: The file is downloaded

> **Note**
>
> *You can also upload and download complete folders. The easiest thing to do is highlight all files and folders of your finished Web site and upload them.*

You have now learnt to load files onto a server. What else should you take into account? One important subject is upper and lower case letters. Unix servers are sensitive to this. Therefore, you should use a uniform file name convention for all pages of your Web site. We recommend you use lower case throughout. If you have a domain with a host, you should find out what the opening page has to be called. The convention for this is normally *index.htm*. Why is this significant? If a user only indicates their domain name in the form `www.domain.co.uk`, the server does not know which file is to be called up first. Therefore the server administrator defines the possible file names for this first file.

Registering your site with search engines

Your page is now on the Net. Friends and acquaintances have already been informed. Now you must beat your drum a little louder. In addition to expensive ways of advertising such as banners (see the next section) you should, before you do anything else, register your Web site with the most important search engines.

Roughly speaking there are three kinds of search engine:

- Active search engines are the classics such as Altavista, Google and Lycos. They work with so-called robots which actively go through the Web. One should make use of this option, so that the robot continues to appear for the foreseeable future.

- Web catalogues subdivide the indexed pages into categories. In most cases this is done by hand. Therefore the Web catalogues also have fewer entries than active search engines and the quality of the collected pages is better. In any case you should register with Web catalogues, such as Yahoo and Hotbot.

- Meta search engines search several active engines and Web catalogues. No registration is required here since meta search engines fall back on data of the other search engines.

Registering with active search engines

The registration procedure with active search engines is different for every one. We will register our site Fireball as an example.

1 Call up the Altavista Web site `www.altavista.co.uk`.

2 At the bottom left of the home page you will find the link ADD YOUR WEB SITE TO ALTAVISTA (see Figure 12.8). Click on this.

Figure 12.8: Click on the link ADD YOUR WEB SITE TO ALTAVISTA, to register your site

3 Next you are presented with a form in which you can give the URL (see Figure 12.9) of your Web site. Confirm this with ADD YOUR WEB SITE TO ALTAVISTA URL.

Figure 12.9: Registering a URL

Tip

On the registration page of a URL you will find a link to the Meta tag generator (see Figure 12.10). This is a form in which you can give information such as the author, description of the site and key words. The HTML source code is then issued with the <META> tag.

Figure 12.10: The meta tag generator of Domains2Trade

Caution

You should not register a Web site with a search engine more than once. The danger of being removed from the index increases by doing so. Have patience: Altavista, for example, is well known for taking a long time to register Web sites, so check on it from time to time.

269

Registering with Web catalogues

In principle, registration with Web catalogues works in a similar way to active search engines. The only difference is that, with Web catalogues, you have to choose one or more categories in which your site will be listed.

We will use Yahoo as the example:

1 Call up Yahoo's home page (www.yahoo.com).

2 In the bottom area you will find the link How to Suggest a Site. You cannot register your site with this link (see Figure 12.11).

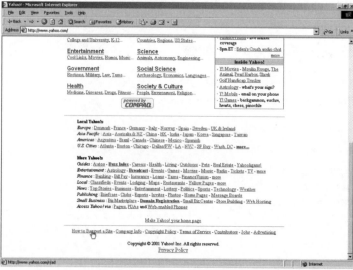

Figure 12.11: You only get a description with this link, so you cannot register a site

3 To register the site you have to put it into a sub-category. For this example we have chosen the category Computer and Internet/Programming_Languages.

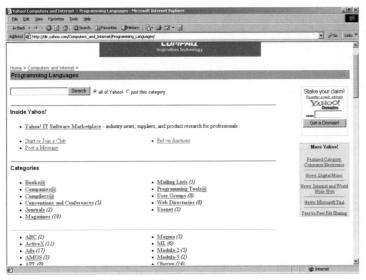

Figure 12.12: At the bottom right you will find a link to register your site in a category

At the bottom right of the sub-category page you will find the link SUGGEST A SITE... This is where you nominate a category for your site (see Figure 12.12).

4 Before you can finally register your site you are asked whether your site is already listed in the directory of Yahoo and whether you have read the information. Make sure you do both of these things. You can then return to the registration procedure by pressing the button BACK TO STEP ONE.

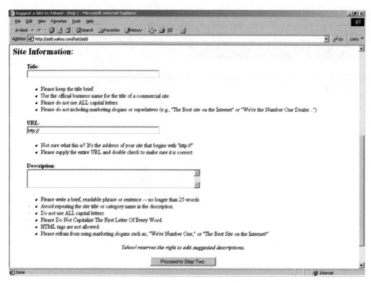

Figure 12.13: Step One of the registration procedure

5 In Step One, check the category again. Then you have to give a short, concise title, the URL, and a description of your Web site. If you have done all this, go on to Step Two.

Note

The details in Figure 12.13 correspond to the information in the meta tags. Nevertheless you have to give all the details again here.

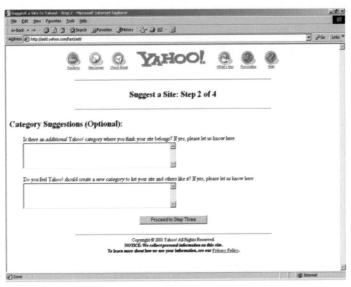

Figure 12.14: In Step Two indicate another category or recommend Yahoo to create a new one

6 In Step Two (see Figure 12.14) you can choose another category in addition to the one already chosen.

> **Note**
> *You don't have to choose a second category, however if another category appears at all relevant, you should select it.*

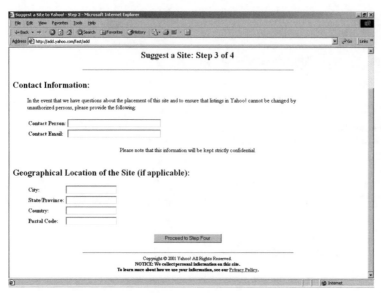

Figure 12.15: You enter the contact information in Step Three

7 Step Three is to enter the contact information. The name of the town is useful if you want to indicate the address of the company.

> **Note**
>
> *Contact information is used as security in Yahoo, so that there are no bogus sites in the catalogue.*

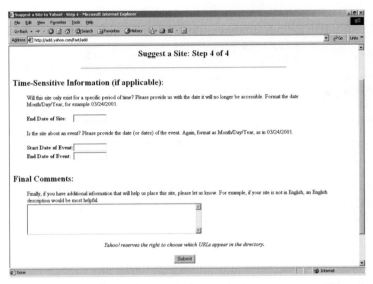

Figure 12.16: Finally you have to indicate whether your page will lose its topicality

8 In the fourth and final step you indicate whether your site will go out of date, or whether it will only stay on line for a certain amount of time (see Figure 12.16). In the comments at the end you can make some personal remarks.

9 At the end, click on SEND.

Several registrations in one go

Of course it is expensive and time consuming to register a site with all available search engines, or even simply those in English. There are services and programs which do this automatically. Out of these, some are free of charge, some are not. For example, we will use Addme, a free service.

> **Note**
> *Why should one register manually if it can be done automatically? Mainly because manual results are normally better and more accurate. There is no automated service that can show the most varied registration procedures correctly.*

The registration procedure with Addme in search engines is as follows:

1 Call up the home page under www.addme.com (see Figure 12.17).

2 In the navigation bar go to the link FREE SEARCH ENGINE SUBMISSION. You will find the link in the middle of the home page.

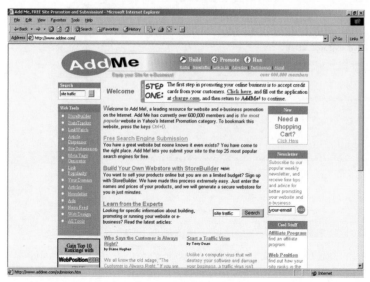

Figure 12.17: Go to FREE SEARCH ENGINE SUBMISSION in the main body of the site

3 In the registration page enter the SITE TITLE, SITE URL, E-MAIL ADDRESS and then click CONTINUE (see Figure 12.18).

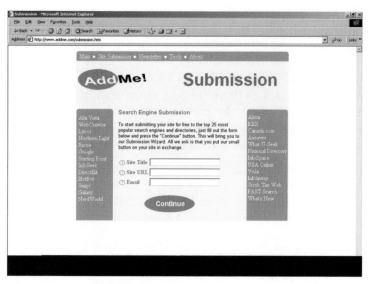

Figure 12.18: Enter the details here

4 If you have entered your web site URL, you will see a new registration form (see Figure 12.19). You indicate your name and other data here.

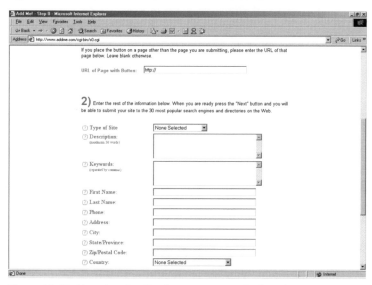

Figure 12.19: You give details of your name and other data in a registration form

5 Once you have entered your details and clicked on NEXT there will be a series of pages where you select which search engines you want to belong to.

Banner advertising

In principle the following is true: Those who can afford it, those who advertise their Web sites with banners. These do not always have to cost money. It is almost impossible for small Web sites, in particular, to create adverts or buy banner space. However there are banner exchange programmes. Lots of small sites take part in this kind of programme. Everyone provides banner space, and your own banner is shown on other sites who are part of the programme, and *vice versa*.

An example of a banner exchange programme is LinkExchange (see Figure 12.20). This service was taken over by Microsoft some time ago. So under the URL www.linkexchange.com you tend to find adverts for Microsoft. If you look under adnetwork.bcentral.com, however, the original banner exchange programme is still available.

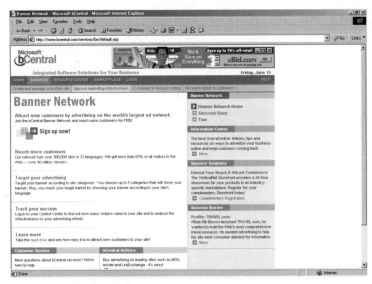

Figure 12.20: LinkExchange

Registration proceeds in the following way:

1 Select the link SIGNUP NOW. First you have to read the terms and conditions.

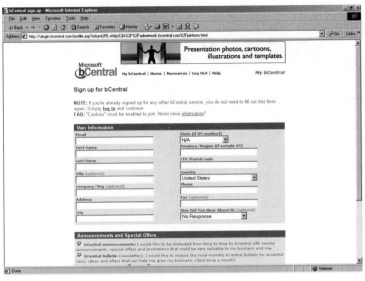

Figure 12.21: Fill in the registration form

2 Then fill in the registration form (see figure 12.21).

3 Now you have to give details about your pages (see figure 12.22).

Caution

Many pages, such as erotic services, are not accepted.

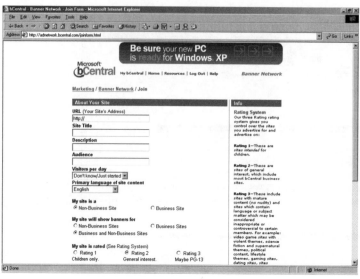

Figure 12.22: Details about the Web site are given here

4 If you confirm at this point, your details are summarised again. After you have accepted everything, you are given a membership number.

5 Now go to the link LOG IN. You can enter your source code into the field for registered users. If you have done this, upload another advertising banner.

Appendix

Questions and answers

What is the difference between HTML 3.2, HTML 4.0 and HTML 4.01?
HTML 3.2 was published in 1996. HTML 4.0 was published in December 1997 in order to expand HTML 3.2 with respect to elements such as frames (although browsers supported this a long time before this). HTML 4.01 was published on Christmas Eve in 1999 and overcame problems faced by HTML 4.0.

Can I use HTML tags in a `<TITLE>` element?
No, it doesn't achieve anything. You can use entities though.

I want to create a distance by means of several `<P></P>` blocks but this doesn't work correctly. Is there a trick?
Many browsers leave out empty paragraphs. Use line breaks (`<BR>`) or put in a non breaking space between the `<P>` elements such as `<P> </P>`.

I know that in numbered lists, elements in the second level are not automatically numbered. How are they numbered then?
You must number them manually. So that the layout matches you have to use invisible tables with numbering in the left column, text in the right.

Is there an option to indicate a link on a FTP-Server and in the process provide the username but not the password (so the user must enter this himself)?
Yes: link to `ftp://username@ftp.servername.net`.

I don't want a graphic to be visible (for example the number of visitors to the site). The instruction of `WIDTH="0" HEIGHT="0"` in the `<IMG>` tag does not give the desired effect. What can I do?
An instruction of 0 for the height and width is not possible. By using `WIDTH="1" HEIGHT="1"`, the graphic is hardly visible.

How can I align the contents of an HTML page in the browser to the centre, and also horizontally and vertically?

Use a table which surrounds the entire contents of the browser, and align the contents in a cell to the centre both horizontally and vertically as follows:

```
<TABLE WIDTH="100%" HEIGHT="100%" BORDER="0"
       CELLPADDING="0" CELLSPACING="0">
<TR>
<TD ALIGN="center" VALIGN="middle">
  <!-- The contents come here -->
</TD>
</TR>
</TABLE>
```

I have seen unordered lists in the Web which have not used the rings of `<UL>`, but bright points. How does this work?

This was almost certainly an invisible table with two columns: one column containing the bullet points (as graphics), and the other the text. Here is a model:

```
<TABLE BORDER="0" CELLPADDING="0" CELLSPACING="0">
<TR>
  <TD><IMG SRC="ring.gif" HSPACE="10"></TD>
  <TD>bullet point 1</TD>
</TR>
<TR>
  <TD><IMG SRC="ring.gif" HSPACE="10"></TD>
  <TD>bullet point 2</TD>
</TR>
</TABLE>
```

Can I check the whole of the form before it is sent?

Unfortunately this is only possible with JavaScript, or with the CGI-Program, with which you are sending it out. The form sending service introduced in Chapter 8 can do this.

Can I suddenly change the content of two frames?
As a rule, no, unless you use JavaScript. Sometimes, it also permits both frames to be inside one frameset. Then you only have to replace the frameset.

HTML entities

The table below lists codes for various special characters.

Source: `www.w3.org/TR/html4/sgml/entities.html`

Special characters

Character	Description	shortened form	Unicode
	non-breaking space	` `	` `
¢	cent	`&cent;`	`&#162;`
£	pound	`&pound;`	`&#163;`
¥	yen	`&yen;`	`&#165;`
§	section sign	`&sect;`	`&#167;`
¨	umlaut	`&uml;`	`&#168;`
©	copyright sign	`&copy;`	`&#169;`
ª	feminine ordinal	`&ordf;`	`&#170;`
»	French left-angle quote	`&laquo;`	`&#171;`
-	hyphen	`&shy;`	`&#173;`
®	registered trademark sign	`&reg;`	`&#174;`
°	degree sign	`&deg;`	`&#176;`
±	plus or minus	`&plusmn;`	`&#177;`
2	superscript 2	`&sup2;`	`&#178;`
3	superscript 3	`&sup3;`	`&#179;`
´	acute accent	`&acute;`	`&#180;`
µ	micron sign	`&micro;`	`&#181;`

Character	Description	shortened form	Unicode
¶	paragraph sign	&para;	&#182;
·	dot	&middot;	&#183;
¸	cedilla	&cedil;	&#184;
1	superscript 1	&sup1;	&#185;
º	masculine ordinal	&ordm;	&#186;
1/4	quarter	&frac14;	&#188;
1/2	half	&frac12;	&#189;
3/4	three quarters	&frac34;	&#190;
À	A with grave accent	&Agrave;	&#192;
Á	A with acute accent	&Aacute;	&#193;
Â	A with circumflex	&Acirc;	&#194;
Ã	A with tilde	&Atilde;	&#195;
Ä	A with umlaut	&Auml;	&#196;
Å	A with ring	&Aring;	&#197;
Æ	AE dipthong	&AElig;	&#198;
Ç	C with cedilla	&Ccedil;	&#199;
È	E with grave accent	&Egrave;	&#200;
É	E with acute accent	&Eacute;	&#201;
Ê	E with circumflex accent	&Ecirc;	&#202;
Ë	E with umlaut	&Euml;	&#203;
Ì	I with grave accent	&Igrave;	&#204;
Í	I with acute accent	&Iacute;	&#205;
Î	I with circumflex accent	&Icirc;	&#206;
Ï	I with umlaut	&Iuml;	&#207;

Character	Description	shortened form	Unicode
Ñ	N with tilde	&Ntilde;	&#209;
Ò	O with grave accent	&Ograve;	&#210;
Ó	O with acute accent	&Oacute;	&#211;
Ô	O with circumflex accent	&Ocirc;	&#212;
Õ	O with tilde	&Otilde;	&#213;
Ö	O with umlaut	&Ouml;	&#214;
x	multiplication sign	&times;	&#215;
Ø	O with slash	&Oslash;	&#216;
Ù	U with grave accent	&Ugrave;	&#217;
Ú	U with acute accent	&Uacute;	&#218;
Û	U with circumflex accent	&Ucirc;	&#219;
Ü	U with umlaut	&Uuml;	&#220;
Ý	Y with acute accent	&Yacute;	&#221;
ß	ß (beta)	&szlig;	&#223;
à	a with grave accent	&agrave;	&#224;
á	a with acute accent	&aacute;	&#225;
â	a with circumflex accent	&acirc;	&#226;
ã	a with tilde	&atilde;	&#227;
ä	a with umlaut	&auml;	&#228;
å	a with ring	&aring;	&#229;
æ	ae ligature	&aelig;	&#230;
ç	c with cedilla	&ccedil;	&#231;
è	e with grave accent	&egrave;	&#232;
é	e with acute accent	&eacute;	&#233;
ê	e with circumflex accent	&ecirc;	&#234;

285

Character	Description	shortened form	Unicode
ë	e with umlaut	&euml;	&#235;
ì	i with grave accent	&igrave;	&#236;
í	i with acute accent	&iacute;	&#237;
î	i with circumflex accent	&icirc;	&#238;
ï	i with umlaut	&iuml;	&#239;
ñ	n with tilde	&ntilde;	&#241;
ò	o with grave accent	&ograve;	&#242;
ó	o with acute accent	&oacute;	&#243;
ô	o with circumflex accent	&ocirc;	&#244;
õ	o with tilde	&otilde;	&#245;
ö	o with umlaut	&ouml;	&#246;
÷	division sign	&divide;	&#247;
ø	o with slash	&oslash;	&#248;
ù	u with grave accent	&ugrave;	&#249;
ú	u with acute accent	&uacute;	&#250;
û	u with circumflex accent	&ucirc;	&#251;
ü	u with umlaut	&uuml;	&#252;
ý	y with acute accent	&yacute;	&#253;
ÿ	y with umlaut	&yuml;	&#255;
€	Euro	&euro;	&#8364;

The Greek alphabet

Character	Description	Shortened form	Unicode
A	capital alpha	Α	913
B	capital beta	Β	914
G	capital gamma	Γ	915
D	capital delta	Δ	916
E	capital epsilon	Ε	917
Z	capital zeta	Ζ	918
H	capital eta	Η	919
Q	capital theta	Θ	920
I	capital iota	Ι	921
K	capital kappa	Κ	922
L	capital lambda	Λ	923
M	capital mu	Μ	924
N	capital nu	Ν	925
J	capital xi	Ξ	926
O	capital omicron	Ο	927
P	capital pi	Π	928
R	capital rho	Ρ	929
S	capital sigma	Σ	931
T	capital tau	Τ	932
Y	capital upsilon	Υ	933
F	capital phi	Φ	934
X	capital chi	Χ	935
C	capital psi	Ψ	936
V	capital omega	Ω	937

Character	Description	Shortened form	Unicode
a	lower case alpha	&alpha;	945
b	lower case beta	&beta;	946
g	lower case gamma	&gamma;	947
d	lower case delta	&delta;	948
e	lower case epsilon	&epsilon;	949
z	lower case zeta	&zeta;	950
h	lower case eta	&eta;	951
u	lower case theta	&theta;	952
i	lower case iota	&iota;	953
k	lower case kappa	&kappa;	954
l	lower case lambda	&lambda;	955
m	lower case mu	&mu;	956
n	lower case nu	&nu;	957
j	lower case xi	&xi;	958
o	lower case omicro	&omicron;	959
π	lower case pi	&pi;	960
ρ	lower case rho	&rho;	961
β	Sigma	&sigmaf;	962
σ	lower case sigma	&sigma;	963
τ	lower case tau	&tau;	964
ψ	lower case upsilon	&upsilon;	965

Character	Description	Shortened form	Unicode
ω	lower case phi	φ	966
ξ	lower case chi	χ	967
χ	lower case psi	ψ	968
ϖ	lower case omega	ω	

Glossary

Anchor
See *Text marks*.

Attribute
A *Tag* can have one or more attributes assigned to it. Every attribute has a *value*.

Background
In HTML you can define a background for a page. This consists of either a colour or an image.

Banner
Form of advertising on the *Web*. Banners are usually shown at the top or at the bottom of a Web site and encourage the user to click on the advertiser's page.

Banner exchange
Smaller Web sites exchange banners with each other. A well known representative of this market is LinkExchange.

Browser
See *Web browser*.

CGI
Common Gateway Interface. A transfer protocol or interface for server-page scripts. Programming language created in the same way as Perl.

CSS
Cascading Stylesheet. Format for *stylesheets* where files have the ending .css.

Domain
Unambiguous name for a *Web site* such as www.domain.co.uk.

Flash
Vector graphic format of Macromedia, which has gained acceptance on the Internet as an unofficial standard.

Form

Input mask in which the user can put his details. A form can consist of different elements such as check boxes, drop-down menus, and text boxes. Forms are usually sent using *CGI* scripts.

Frame

A *Web page* is divided into several parts, for example a navigation bar and a contents frame. Each of these parts is a separate HTML page and is independent from the rest of the scrollbar. They are called frames.

FTP

File Transfer Protocol. Transfer protocol for data with which you can load your *Web site* onto a *Webserver*.

GIF

CompuServe Graphics Interchange. Originally from the image format developed by CompuServe which is used on the Internet. It only supports 256 colours, but can contain a transparent colour. In addition a *GIF-Animation* can be saved in this format.

GIF animation

A sequence of single images are saved in the *GIF* format as an animation. The animation can be slowed down and played once, several times, or an unlimited number of times.

Hexadecimal

Notation of colours in *HTML*; for example #FFFFFF for white. The model works in the following way: the double sharp # highlights the start of the colour notation. In many Photoshop dialogues it is missing. The next two figures indicate the *RGB colour system* red value, the following two the green value, and the last two, the blue value. The value is calculated by multiplying the first figure by 16 and then adding the second figure. In order to be able to show 256 values, every figure has to be able to accept 16 values, therefore the range of values of a figure is not enough. Alternatively 0 to 9 and A (10) to F (15) are used. FF is therefore 15 x 16 = 240. Then the second F = 15 is added and from this comes the value of 255 for white.

Home page

The start page of a *Web site*.

Hosts
Providers of space on a *Web server*. Most hosts also support their own *Domains*. This means that your Web site can be obtained at `www.domain.co.uk`.

HTML
Hypertext Markup Language. The page description language for Web pages. HTML contains *Tags* (commands), which are interpreted by the browser one at a time. This book is all about HTML.

HTTP
Hypertext Transfer Protocol. Transfer protocol for data on the *Web*. HTML pages can be transferred using HTTP.

Image map
Function contained in *HTML* which allows you to divide an image into several areas and provide each area with a *Link* or other functions. The *Tag* (command) for an Imagemap in *HTML* is `<MAP>`, for an area it is `<AREA>`.

Indexed colours
Colours which are combined in a colour palette and are cut from a large colour space can have a maximum of 256 colours. Every colour value has its own index which determines its place in the palette. Indexed colours are mainly used when something is saved in the *GIF* file format.

Interlaced
Saving option for *GIF, JPEG* and *PNG* files. The files are built in the browser in several stages. In *GIF,* only every eighth row is shown at first. In *JPEG* and *PNG* the file is shown from blurry to sharp.

Internet
Global computer net. Contains several services like *FTP* and the *World Wide Web.*

Internet Explorer
The web browser of Microsoft. It is found in version 5.5 SP1. Internet Explorer can also interpret new HTML commands which do not comply to the *W3C* standard.

Java
Programming language originally developed by Sun which can be executed independently from the platform. A virtual machine is necessary for this.

JavaScript
Programming language which is interpreted by the *Web browser*. JavaScript is an addition to *HTML* that was established by *Netscape*. JavaScript contains important functions such as loops and variables used for programming.

JPEG
Joint Picture Experts Group. File format for the *Web*. JPEG has a lossy compression and is useful for photos and graphics with lots of layers of colour.

Link
Reference from one Web site to another. A link can be made relative (e.g. `../images`) or absolute (`www.pearsoned.com`).

Mozilla
Open source project, which is the basis for the new *Netscape* browser (Netscape 6). It is special because the source code stays open and everyone can take part in the development. The current situation can be examined under `www.mozilla.org`.

Netscape
Browser manufacturer recently bought by AOL. The *Web browser* Netscape Navigator is programmed by this. This is available in Version 6.

Opera
A web browser. This runs a distant second to *Internet Explorer* and *Netscape Navigator*.

PNG
Format for images on the Web. It was originally developed in order to get round copyright problems with the *GIF* format, but has now been developed beyond *GIF*. It supports 256 colours as PNG-8, and even 16 million as PNG-24. PNGs are compressed loss free with LZW and allow transparency as well as animation.

RGB colour system
RGB stands for red, green and blue. The RGB system joins the three colour channels together to form colours. It is used by monitors.

SGML
Standard Generalized Markup Language. This description language forms the basis of *HTML* and also *XML*.

Stylesheet

Stylesheets are used to format and position elements in HTML pages. What is special about stylesheets is that a definition can be modified once in a central position and can then be used on different areas.

For stylesheets a special language has to be used. In normal HTML pages this is *CSS*. For *XML* the stylesheet language is called *XSL*.

Table

A table in *HTML* consists of rows containing cells. In addition to the classic use as a layout element, tables can also be used for positioning objects and structuring a *Web page*.

Tag

A *HTML* command is called a tag. Most tags consist of a start tag and an end tag.

Text marks

Reference within an HTML page. You define the place to which you want to jump with an anchor. You refer to this with a link and an appended #.

Transparent GIF

A *GIF* graphic that consists of a single colour which is switched to transparent. Used frequently in tables as a dummy and for positioning.

URL

Uniform Resource Locator. The *Internet* address that you have to give in a link, for example `www.pearsoned.com`.

W3C

World Wide Web Consortium. Consortium for the finding and establishment of Internet standards such as HTML 4.01. The W3C is found under the address `www.w3c.org`.

Web

The World Wide Web (WWW or W3) is the graphics part of the *Internet*. In order to be able to view the pages of the World Wide Web you need a *Web browser* which interprets *HTML* pages.

Web browser

The Web browser displays the *HTML* pages. It interprets the *HTML* code and displays the page and graphics. With Plug-Ins, which are usually attached, you can also display additional formats such as *Flash*.

Web page

Individual HTML pages with accompanying images. For the most part a web page is a *Web site*.

Web server

Computer which is permanently connected to the *Internet*. With the *URL*, every user can access *Web pages* on the Web server with an *Internet* connection. To load data on the Web server *FTP* is normally used.

Web-safe colours

Colour palette with 216 colours which are both on the Macintosh and in Windows. If you use these you can be sure that the user can display them correctly. The web safe colour palette was originally developed by the browser manufacturer *Netscape*.

Web site

A Web site consists of several Web pages. The start page is described as a *Home page*.

Value

The value is the information which is assigned to an *attribute*. A value can consist of numbers or characters, depending on the kind of *attribute*.

XHTML

Extensible Hypertext Markup Language. The standardisation of *HTML to XML* guide lines is summarised under this generic term.

XML

Extensible Markup Language. Structuring language for documents on the Web. The standard is maintained by *W3C*.

XSL

Extensible Stylesheet Language. A language created in *XML* for *stylesheets*.

Index

CSS (cascading stylesheets) language 201, 291, 295
– *see also* stylesheets

D

DATE 259
definitions lists 77-80
DESCRIPTION 258
directory paths 89-94
disc symbols 62-4
dithering 111
DIV 39-40
DL tag 77-80
Domains2Trade 269
domains 291
downloading browsers 6-12
downloading files 99
drop-down menus 175, 188-90

E

editors 12-14
email 97-9
– sending forms by 195-8
ENCTYPE 178
end-tags 18, 19
entities 22, 283-6
– non-breaking spaces 22, 31-2, 36
external links 94
external stylesheets 206-10

F

feedback forms 174
files
– downloading 99
– formats 110-13
– loading onto servers 261-6
– names 89-90
– uploading 190-1
Flash 291
flashing test 43, 48
fonts 48-57
– colour codes 53-7, 292
– and heading levels 42
– monospaced 43
– size 51-3

– stylesheet attributes 218-21
– typeface 49-50
– *see also* formatting
footnotes 47
formatting
– characters 43-8
– frames in Web pages 246-51
– heading levels 41-3
– links 86-8
– lists 80-3
– logical formatting 40-1
– physical formatting 40-1
– STRONG 40-1
– tables 138-45, 151-2
– *see also* fonts
forms 174-200, 292
– ACTION 178
– buttons 192-4
– check boxes 184-6
– ENCTYPE 178
– frames 177-8
– invisible fields 192
– menus 175, 188-90
– METHOD 178
– multi-row text fields 182-4
– password fields 180-1
– radio buttons 186-8
– resetting 193
– sending 194-200
– text fields 176-7, 178-80, 182-4
– uploading files 190-1
– uses 174-7
FRAME, attribute values for 143-5
frames, for forms 177-8
frames, stylesheet attributes 227-31
frames, for tables 139-40, 143-5
frames in Web pages 234-56, 292
– advantages 255
– allocating files to 236
– borders 249-51
– defining framesets 234
– disadvantages 255
– fixed representation 238-41
– formatting 246-51
– height 238-42
– horizontal/vertical divisions 235-7